Samuel Bailey

On the Received Text of Shakespeare's Dramatic Writings

And its Improvement

Samuel Bailey

On the Received Text of Shakespeare's Dramatic Writings
And its Improvement

ISBN/EAN: 9783337055998

Printed in Europe, USA, Canada, Australia, Japan

Cover: Foto ©Thomas Meinert / pixelio.de

More available books at **www.hansebooks.com**

ON THE RECEIVED TEXT OF SHAKESPEARE'S DRAMATIC WRITINGS AND ITS IMPROVEMENT

BY

SAMUEL BAILEY

LONDON
LONGMAN, GREEN, LONGMAN, AND ROBERTS
1862

LONDON

PRINTED BY SPOTTISWOODE AND CO.

NEW-STREET SQUARE

PREFACE.

—♦—

The Notes on Shakespeare which compose the present Volume were begun as a diversion from abstruser studies; but the Author soon found that to do anything effectual in this way required nearly as much diligent research and patient thought as to discuss the Principles of Value, the Metaphysics of Vision, or the Theory of Reasoning. The attractiveness of the employment, nevertheless, drew him on, till his memoranda had, in the progress of years, accumulated to a considerable bulk, from which he now offers a selection to the Public. Should it turn out that he has succeeded in throwing light on any portion of the text of our great dramatist, it will be no small addition to the pleasure he has already enjoyed in making the attempt.

Norbury, near Sheffield.
Nov. 21st, 1861.

CONTENTS.

ON THE TEXT OF SHAKESPEARE.

PART I.

PRINCIPLES.

It is too well known to be more than glanced at here by way of introduction to what follows, that no great writer in the English language has been so unfortunate in regard to the imperfect state in which his productions were given to the world as Shakespeare.

The defectiveness of the text in the dramatic works appears, from the scanty evidence we possess, to have been partly occasioned by the slovenly manner in which many of them were first taken down from the lips, or copied from the manuscript notes of the players, or from the prompters' books; and partly by the no less slovenly manner in which they were printed. But even such slovenliness would have had no permanent consequences had not the author himself, in the latter part of his life, when he might have set all right, shown an unaccountable, or at least an extraordinary, disregard and carelessness about the printing of his own works. A genuine text cannot be said indeed ever to have existed in print. The actual corruption of it even in the best early editions is conspicuous in the numerous efforts subsequently made to amend or restore it.

Sometimes the suggestions offered with this view have been so felicitous that they have been instantaneously adopted. At other times the proposed emendations have thrown no light except on the weakness of the proposers. They have been too often mere random guesses hastily thrown out, while surely the importance of a right text should have commanded the patient and considerate application of recognised, or at all events systematic, canons. To some of our best commentators however these derogatory strictures may but occasionally apply, and it is readily acknowledged that we are indebted to their labours for the removal of many blemishes. Still there is a prevailing want of explicit methodical procedure. In determining whether any passage is corrupt, and in devising or testing any emendations of the received text, we ought alike to proceed, as every thoughtful critic will admit, on definite principles. To lay down such principles is doubtless a task of some difficulty, and we cannot therefore feel surprised that it has not been hitherto formally attempted; or at any rate satisfactorily accomplished; although they perhaps might be collected in some measure from the practice as well as comments of our most judicious annotators: but without disparagement to what has been done, there is ample room, I conceive, for a further effort in the same direction.

I purpose, therefore, in the present treatise, first to consider the grounds on which any passage can be rightly pronounced corrupt, and secondly to suggest the conditions to be fulfilled in any emendations brought forward with a view to restore the reading to its original purity. Concurrently and subsequently I shall adduce numerous illustrative instances of the principles explained and enforced.

It is to be borne in mind that what I have to say on these points is in special reference to the works of Shakespeare, and may or may not be applicable to the productions of other writers of inferior ability and in a dissimilar position.

The principal circumstances which lead us to to suspect and justify us in deeming any passage in his Plays to be corrupt appear to be the following:—

1. Rhythmical and grammatical errors. Of the first may be mentioned a limping in the metre not disappearing even when the passage is read with due consideration of all the peculiarities of pro-

nunciation, accent, and rhythm belonging to the times, or habitual to the writer.

These circumstances have been so copiously illustrated by preceding writers of the last age, and more recently by Mr. Sydney Walker, that I have no need to do more than refer to their works for an exposition both of the peculiarities of pronunciation, which are to be taken into account, and of the metrical errors not emanating from the author which require correction.

The grammatical errors are (chiefly, at least) such faults of syntax as cannot be accounted for on similar contemporaneous or personal grounds.

2. Discordance in the sentiments or in the language with the character of the dramatic speaker — a circumstance so rarely brought forward as a mark of corruption in the text that a bare mention of it is sufficient.

3. Discordance in the sentiments or in the language with the habitual mode of thinking or with the habitual phraseology of the author himself.

4. The repetition, without some assignable cause or purpose, of a word or phrase in such close proximity as to be displeasing to ordinary taste. This is a defect of very frequent occurrence in the received text, and unless we suppose Shakespeare to have been destitute of a sensibility in this respect which is possessed by very common-place people, we must consider it as a mark of corruption. Nevertheless as there are repetitions that are per-

fectly genuine, great care is occasionally required to discriminate the authentic from the spurious, and on account of the importance of a right discrimination between them I purpose to offer some considerations on the subject in a separate chapter. To do it here would occupy a disproportionate space.

5. No-meaning or nonsense or absurdity—a defect obvious at once to everybody. Should it indeed not be obvious the case will fall under one or other of the ensuing heads.

6. Irrelevancy, or want of significant appropriateness in a sentence or expression. The phrase may have a clear meaning in itself and be quite Shakespearian, but seems out of place where it is, alien to the context, does not help on the dialogue, nor elucidate the drift of the speaker.

Of this I purpose to point out an example in Hamlet's soliloquy, when that celebrated passage is under review and one in the "Tempest," not to mention instances in other plays.

7. Incoherence, or want of congruity or consistency in the thoughts, or of consecutiveness in the reasoning, except when these defects are purposely introduced as characteristic of the speaker; as in the case, for example, of Mistress Quickly or neighbour Dogberry. Such faults are, it appears to me, of unappreciated value in the determination of spuriousness. The circumstances set forth under the six preceding heads, although of very unequal

importance, may all in their turn form serviceable criteria of corruption in the received text; but it is to defects coming under the present head that I am more expressly desirous of calling attention as constituting a criterion the application of which is likely to be fruitful in happy results, if conducted with caution and patience. The defects in question may for brevity's sake be summed up in the inadequate phrase *incoherence of thought*, and a few words may not be wasted in explaining and elucidating on what grounds and in what manner it is intended to be employed as an index of spuriousness.

The writings of a first-rate author exhibit amongst their conspicuous characteristics definiteness of aim, not only in the whole compass of what he is about but in each separate part; firmness and consistency of thought, and consecutiveness of reasoning: characteristics which, when manifested in verbal expression, always imply precision of language and cannot well be dissociated from it. A master of composition expresses himself in exact terms, sets clearly before us the positions he takes up; gives us metaphors which are neither mixed nor misapplied; similes which are not unlike; antitheses clearly brought out; general propositions which are not confused, incongruous, or wavering; trains of reasoning carried out to their proper conclusions without being diverted from their course by irrelevant topics.

The inferior writer, on the other hand, shows

indeterminateness of purpose; is full of incoherent thoughts and inconsistent figures; comparisons not obvious and contrasts that miscarry; he starts in a certain direction and loses himself by the way; sets himself to illustrate one proposition, and ends by holding up his feeble and flickering light to another.

Such not being the characteristics of a remarkably strong-minded writer like Shakespeare, it is plain that when we find any of them intruding into his composition, under the admitted circumstances that it has been irregularly taken down, has not had the benefit of his personal supervision, and is in consequence full of acknowledged inaccuracies, we may not only reasonably suspect, but feel a confident assurance that we have not the genuine reading before us.

At the same time such criteria as these require to be applied with reference to the peculiarities visible in Shakespeare as in all great writers. While his works exhibit a sagacious and vigorous mind, so that we expect from him nothing confused or incongruous, or weak, or wavering, they also manifest a proneness to condensation, an impatience of diffuseness that seems as if it would crush meaning into the smallest possible compass, and a consequent and corresponding brevity of language; qualities which are generally attended with admirable effects, but which, as they are apt to lead to harsh and constrained expressions, occasionally darken his composition except to a closely attentive reader, and now and then even to the ablest and most patient of his admirers.*

The obscurity in question is enhanced by an occasional tinge of what may be called pedantry, whether personal or belonging to the age; a use of terms in an etymological and hence somewhat strained acceptation. An appropriate meaning is perhaps fully expressed on such occasions, but it is far from being obvious to a reader fresh to the uncommon application of the words, and not competent to trace the derivation.

As nevertheless an apt and even forcible sense exempt from intrinsic incongruity may generally be discovered, we have to be careful not to confound the impediments so arising to an immediate apprehension of his drift, with the obscurity, incoherence, and confusion fathered upon him by the blunders of reporters, copyists, and printers — a discrimination doubtless at times exceedingly difficult.

Another characteristic tending to disturb our conclusions from internal evidence as to what is and what is not genuine in the received text, is our author's besetting propensity, in season and out of season, to play upon words. Occasionally this leads him into ill-timed puerilities, far-fetched con-

* Even Mr. Hallam, accustomed as he was to all kinds of style complains of "the extreme obscurity of Shakespeare's diction." — *Literature of Europe*, vol. iii. p. 92.

ceits, and jests not of unquestionable "prosperity," which, if we set out from any postulate of his undeviating good taste, uniform strong sense, and complete mastery of his art,—in a word, his unfaltering excellence—we should be compelled to condemn as spurious; but which are saved from that fate by the way in which the manifestations of the propensity are interwoven with some of the best parts of his composition.

It must also be allowed, along with the preceding defects, that our great dramatic poet sometimes swells out into bombast, and, while still maintaining his clearness and vigour, even approaches to rant.

On account of such unfavourable characteristics it is abundantly obvious that we cannot take all deviations from perfection as indicative of corruption in the text; and it may be well for me to guard expressly against the supposition that I design to do so.

No-meaning, irrelevancy of propositions, and incoherence of thought, as I have explained them, are the substantial faults (apart from others of a more formal nature) which I conceive Shakespeare could not commit; which I consider, consequently, as indications of spuriousness in his received text; and which (especially the last) I have set myself to apply in that character.

Whether the tests I have proposed are adequate or not, one thing is clear, that before we proceed to exercise our ingenuity in improving the received text, we ought to have established on satisfactory grounds, or it ought to be unmistakeably manifest without the necessity of proof, that the passage we seek to restore *is* spurious. We are then at the proper starting-place for a quest after the right reading. One would suppose that this preparatory step must be a matter of course and could scarcely be neglected; but it is in truth often carelessly attended to, and sometimes altogether omitted. The eagerness consequent on having a new reading to propose leaps over the inquiry whether there is really any call for it.

An apposite illustration of the light way in which such an essential preliminary is passed over may be found in the Perkins folio. The following lines occur in "Measure for Measure :"

"How would you be,
If He, which is *the top of judgment*, should
But judge you as you are?"

Act ii. sc. 2.

Here where we find complete sense and nothing but Shakespearian language*, there is not the slight-

* The same phrase, *top of judgment*, occurs in Hamlet, act ii. scene 2, and the word top is so often employed by Shakespeare both as a noun and a verb, to express height, climax, or pre-eminence, as to form an almost characteristic phrase. Thus, Salisbury, in "King John," on seeing the dead body of Arthur, exclaims,—

"This is the very *top*,
The height, the crest, or crest unto the crest,
Of murder's arms."

Act iv. sc. 3.

est call for alteration, even if the passage could be altered for the better. Yet the old corrector substitutes *God* for *top*, not only needlessly, but, as it happens, to the injury of the sense.

While the first process, which is thus often lightly attended to by the commentator, as if he were in haste to get to the next, is both necessary and important, we must bear in mind that it only clears the way for the second without advancing it. Suppose that, in the last example, the expression *top of judgment* instead of being arbitrarily assumed to be corrupt had been proved to be so, the establishment of its spuriousness would not have had the slightest tendency to support the proposed substitution of *God of judgment* in its place. The two processes are distinct and require independent attention.

Hence we may completely establish the existence of an error, or it may be so evident as not to require proof, and yet we may be totally unable to supply the correction of it — a position in

Again, in "Antony and Cleopatra," Cæsar, after learning the suicide of the former, apostrophises him as

"my brother, my competitor
In top of all design, my mate in empire."
Act v. sc. 1.

In other places we have, "the spire and top of praises;" "Edward the base shall top the legitimate;" "top of honour;" and a number of similar phrases.

which the critic of Shakespeare is in fact continually liable to be placed.

How the rectification of a faulty passage is in any case to be set about seems hardly an affair of rule or direct prescription. Nevertheless, the considerations which will be hereafter brought forward in support of some of the emendations I have to suggest, will probably afford a few hints and examples not unserviceable to that end. Meanwhile certain conditions may be laid down as indispensably requisite (except under peculiar circumstances) in any emendations proposed to remedy proved or admitted defects. Such, I conceive, are those which I shall immediately proceed to state and explain.

1. The proposed emendation must correct the harshness, incoherence, incongruity, want of meaning, or other defect in the received text, on account of which it is proposed. This condition is self-evidently indispensable, but amongst several emendations which fulfil it, some may do it more completely and more happily than others.

2. It should not be lower in tone of thought or force of expression than the context into which it is to be introduced; nor be in any other way inconsistent with it. This condition is also gradational, or admits of being more or less happily fulfilled.

3. The language of the emendation should be such as Shakespeare can be shown to have habitually

or at least occasionally employed. If this, although highly desirable, cannot be laid down as absolutely imperative in all cases, yet where it is departed from, special reasons should be assigned; and the lowest requirement must exact that the phraseology shall be that of the age in which he wrote, or of books then in current use. While, therefore, a proposed emendation with this lowest qualification would not be necessarily excluded, another emendation expressed in phraseology used elsewhere even sparingly by him would *ceteris paribus* have higher claims to be received; and a third clothed in his habitual language would have higher still.

This condition, therefore, is also gradational, or one the fulfilment of which admits of degrees.

It may be contended, perhaps, in contradiction to one part of this condition that no word ought to be admitted into an emendation which is not found elsewhere in his writings; but this on trial would be seen to be too rigorous.

An example in point is furnished by the correction of *Aristotle's checks* to *Aristotle's Ethics*, which cannot be rejected, notwithstanding the fact that the term *ethics* is not to be found in any other place in the whole range of Shakespeare's dramas. The instance may be considered perhaps as scarcely relevant, since the words may be looked upon as forming the title of a book: but other examples will present themselves as we proceed.* At the

* I may cite the word *counterwait* which I have suggested in "Comedy of Errors."

same time it may be allowed that the introduction of a *notable* term, nowhere used by him, would be *prima facie* suspicious, and even exceptionable in an emendation, or in settling a disputed reading.

For example, the word *tone* does not occur once in his dramatic writings, and its total absence would constitute a presumptive ground of objection to any amendment in which it had a place,—an objection, however, which might be overcome by special circumstances, since that word may be found in Bacon and other contemporary writers. On the whole, the great condition to be exacted is that the language of an emendation shall be the language of Shakespeare in other places ; and every deviation from it must be justified by particular considerations.

4. It is not enough, however, that the three preceding conditions should be fulfilled by a proposed emendation, since they may be so without producing a positive conviction that it is the right one, and they may be satisfied by several rival suggestions. They are all indispensable, but they are not together necessarily sufficient.

An emendation, it is obvious, may completely remedy the defect in view, may be of the proper tone and force, and be couched in Shakespearian language, not only without completely convincing us that it is the exact reading, but without being exclusively successful in those points. Half a dozen other emendations may also fulfil the requirements, and thus so far the right reading will be indeterminate. From such a difficulty, not often occurring perhaps in so extreme a form, there seems to be no escape, unless some further circumstance can be found which is conclusively satisfactory, and which, in the case of rival amendments, gives to one a superiority over the rest.

A fourth condition then must be laid down to the effect that an emendation in order to be received must farther possess or be attended by some attribute or circumstance of this decisive or crucial character, forming a positive title to admission.

A brief glance at the various ways in which wrong readings or spurious passages are occasioned, may show what are the crucial circumstances to look out for, and how far we have the means of complying with the requirements of this fourth condition.

The chief errors of transcribers, writers from dictation or from recitation, short-hand writers, decypherers of short-hand, and compositors, are mistakes of one word or phrase for another in consequence of either similarity of sound, or, when the sight is concerned, of similarity in the forms of the words or of the letters, often incalculably increased by bad handwriting which confounds all forms.*

* The evils flowing from bad handwriting have never been sufficiently appreciated, but few apparently trivial circum-

Other circumstances, nevertheless, besides similarity of sound or of literal shape, occur to vitiate the text.

Some of these are incident to the compositor, such as an accidental mixture of type in his case, or his taking a letter from the wrong compartment, or his eye catching a word in the manuscript from the line above or the line below, or some other part of it, when there is no affinity of any kind between the right word and the supposititious one. He is apt also occasionally to compose a line from his mental conception rather than his sight, which may betray him into a blunder. Sometimes too a word lingers in his eye or his mind after he ought to have done with it, and settles down in a wrong place to the utter discomfiture of the legitimate occupant and its neighbours—an incident likely enough to give rise to that disagreeable repetition

stances have occasioned more mistakes, not only of the press, but in the general affairs of the world, and greater waste of time, than a practice which is so easily avoided by those persons who chiefly fall into it. Physicians' prescriptions are a notorious case in point. At one time (I hope the absurdity has passed away) it was regarded as *low* to write legibly; a prejudice which Hamlet mentions in his account to Horatio of forging certain instructions from the King :—

"I sat me down,
Devised a new commission; wrote it fair.
I once did hold it, as our statists do,
A baseness to write fair, and labour'd much
How to forget that learning." Act v. sc. 2.

of a word in a line or in two proximate lines, which has already been adverted to.

There are errors also incident to dictation and to writing from dictation and to copying from an original draught. Not only is the copyist liable to certain mistakes in common with the compositor, but he sometimes vitiates the text in ways peculiar to himself—ways so subtile and various as to elude description. There is one mode, however, in which the text is apt to be corrupted by him palpable enough to be pointed out, and which has been much more prevalent and influential, I apprehend, than is usually suspected. It occurs when successive copyists or revisers, or the same at successive times, are engaged upon the same text. In this case after an error has once found its way into a manuscript and the manuscript is recopied or revised by a different person or by the same person on different occasions, the second operator discerning that an error exists and being desirous to rectify it makes the attempt not by restoring the original reading, of which he may in fact know nothing, but by altering other neighbouring words to make them tally in scope with the spurious one. Since the word which has been put into the text by mistake obstinately refuses to coalesce with those around it, the re-copyist or reviser, in order to get rid of the palpable discord between them, resorts to the expulsion not of the intruding vocable but of the legitimate words whose harmonious relations to the context have been disturbed. He then follows it up by introducing into their places other words more congenial with the intruder.

In this way blunders have propagated blunders, resulting in a thorough depravation of the text. Several examples of mistakes so engendered will be pointed out in the sequel.

When we take a survey of all these sources of error, the most important feature in the view for our present purpose is that the blunders arising from some of the circumstances enumerated retain some relics of the right reading, and thus assist in their own correction, while others do not. Mistakes founded on resemblance of sounds or similarity of visible appearance supply some clue to the genuine text. If *soil* has been inadvertently substituted for *foil*, the defect in sense shows that we have the wrong word before us, and the resemblance borne to the interloper by a word which removes the defect indicates a high probability that it is the right one. Thus that similarity which was the cause of the error not only aids us in rectifying it, but becomes evidence that the original text has been recovered.

It is when such mistakes have been pointed out and have been so rectified that the proposed emendations have at once commended themselves to universal adoption.

A few apposite examples may serve to corroborate these remarks.

One may be found in the expression of Falstaff's, "so both the *degrees* prevent my curses," rectified by the substitution of *diseases* for *degrees:* a second, in the correction of the line

"Rights by rights *fouler*, strengths by strengths do fail,"

into

Rights by rights *founder:*

a third example is furnished by the passage, "That daughter there of Spain, the lady Blanch, is *near* to England" altered to *niece* to England: and a fourth happy emendation of the same kind presents itself in replacing *knit* by *kin* in the line

"The Earl of Armagnac, near *knit* to Charles."

In every one of these cases we readily discern how the error may have arisen from the resemblance between the original word and that substituted for it; and since the several emendations fit into the text with happy exactness, and are altogether conformable to the conditions prescribed, the conviction produced by the union of these circumstances that we have got hold of the right words is complete.

Thus a main circumstance, not only to guide us in our search, but to determine whether we have found the genuine reading, is the resemblance of a proposed emendation to the received text so marked as to show the way in which the latter supplanted the original. This similarity coming upon the fulfilment of the preceding conditions is usually decisive.

It is different with errors arising from the eye of the compositor or writer catching a wrong word from another line, and from the other inauspicious incidents in copying and printing already described. As such for the most part contain no relics of the original text, they supply no clue to their own rectification, and no means of proving that the genuine phraseology has been found. For example, there can be no doubt that the repetition of *help* in the second of the following lines is spurious, inasmuch as it not merely offends the taste, but is nearly unmeaning. There is scarcely a signification, even faintly, appropriate, to be affixed to the line as it stands :

> "Therefore, merchánt, I'll limit thee this day,
> To seek thy *help* by beneficial *help*."
>
> *Comedy of Errors*, act i. sc. 1.

We feel quite sure that Shakespeare never wrote this : one of the *helps* must be spurious ; but here, as in perhaps most such cases of repetition, we have no reason to suppose the mistake to have originated in similarity, and consequently we have no guide to the right reading in the sound or the visible form of the words.

Hence, with regard to this large class of errors in which resemblance has had no part, we try in vain to find the right reading in similar words. We are at a loss how to proceed both to discover the genuine text and to prove it such when found. There is in these cases no decisive circumstance extrinsic to the sense of the passage to render a proposed emendation quite satisfactory in itself or to single it out as the best amongst rival suggestions. When they equally fulfil the three conditions laid down, namely, remove the defect, maintain the tone of the composition, and speak in Shakespearian language, we can do no more than pronounce the reading indeterminate.

It fortunately happens, however, that very frequently a single suggestion, or some one of the suggestions, when there are several, so completely remedies the fault in the text, and so obviously excels the rest if there are rivals, that every reader unites in receiving it. It is this marked felicity in filling up the vacant place, in such cases, which constitutes our only assurance of having got hold of the original words.

Thus there are two different modes of satisfying the fourth condition requiring in an emendation some crucial or decisive circumstance or attribute. It may be satisfied by (1) similarity in the proposed emendation to the received reading: (2) felicity or completeness in fulfilling the three antecedent conditions, when resemblance is not in question.

These circumstances themselves admit of degrees,

and both may be concerned in the final determination.

Of two emendations equal in point of similarity to the received text, one may be superior in felicity; and conversely of two which are equal in felicity, one may be superior in similarity, in which cases (not very likely to occur) the superiority in whichever point it may be will determine the reading.

In general it will be found, as I have already observed, that there is a marked superiority in some one or other of the proposed corrections; but when it happens that the palm cannot be adjudged to any one of the competitors, we are under no obligation to make the award. They must take their places, for the present at least, under the head of uncertain or doubtful.

In the sequel, I shall bring forward a number of instances to show that with our present lights, equality of claims is not an imaginary case, but of frequent occurrence, leaving the text in many passages wholly indeterminate. Such passages, it is to be hoped, may be gradually reduced in number by the combined efforts of future commentators, and in the meantime it is useful to register them for what they are.

The principles which I have here explained as proper, if not necessary, to guide us in determining whether a passage is corrupt, and in the admission of proposed emendations in the received text of

Shakespeare, are applicable in their whole extent to that great body of corrections for which we are indebted to the celebrated Perkins folio.

It ought to be clearly understood at the outset, and consistently borne in mind in any attempt to appreciate their individual value, that they have no authority properly so-called to back them. They have nothing to stand upon but their own merits. Ignorant as we are of the corrector's name, character, position, and opportunities, and of the motives under which he undertook his laborious task, we cannot ascribe to his alterations in the received text the weight which a knowledge of such personal circumstances might possibly, but by no means necessarily, have conferred. The only weight they can have is that which may be due to their intrinsic qualities, and no course is open to us but to test every one of them by the same *criteria* which we should apply to any emendations proposed by a living commentator of the year 1861.

On this view and this plan of proceeding, the question whether or not they are a modern fabrication becomes of no critical importance; the only points to be established in each case are, whether any fault exists in the received text, and if a fault is shown to exist, whether the proposed emendation fulfils the conditions required in all emendations. If it does, the date of it sinks into a matter of indifference.

It is doubtless always important to the community that any false pretence should be exposed; but beyond a common interest in good morals, the lover of Shakespeare is not in the present case really concerned in the inquiry at what time or with whom the manuscript corrections originated. In the absence of all credentials the corrections in question rank in value just the same, whether they are due to the seventeenth century or to our own age. New or old, forged or genuine, they are what they are, and must stand or fall by their own intrinsic deserts, without any support from the shadow of authority which has been vainly flung over them, and which can only prejudice what it cannot corroborate.

Nor will it do to adopt a middle course: we must either receive the whole on authority, or apply to all of them the same tests which are applied to professedly modern suggestions — there is no medium: for if you select only a part of them for adoption, you will have to show on what grounds you admit some and reject others. Should you allege that you are for admitting such as you consider good and rejecting such as you consider bad, you will be manifestly abandoning authority altogether. You will be wholly relying on your own judgment, and very wisely too, just as you will do in accepting or refusing to accept the emendations proposed in the present treatise. In order to make a proper use of the Perkins folio, it is essential to begin by divesting the mind of all impressions that there is or can be any deference due to it.

It is in the spirit here described that in the following pages I have dealt with these noted manuscript corrections. As a body of hints and suggestions they are exceedingly serviceable, and there are so many corrupt passages in the plays that can scarcely be discussed without referring to the volume that I shall find frequent occasion to advert to it.

It is bare justice to add my impression that, as far as Mr. Collier is concerned, the question of fabrication has been satisfactorily disposed of. I never for my own part could see the slightest ground for such an imputation on him, and always felt in reading his statements that I had to do with a writer of good faith and honourable feeling. It seemed to me certain that any errors he might fall into would be such mistakes in judgment as we are all liable to commit without any moral imputation, not deviations from integrity. These impressions have been amply confirmed by the external evidence which he has been enabled to adduce; but independently of all other considerations, the immense number of manuscript corrections, small and great, renders it wholly incredible that they should have been the work of any one bent on deceit and fraudulence. There could be no adequate purpose in the view of an unprincipled writer to induce him to undertake the enormous labour of such a fabrication. No honour and no emolument could be procured by it; or if any of either could be expected, the talent and diligence required for the invention of such a body of corrections (good, bad, and indifferent as they are) would have achieved far higher fame, and obtained far greater remuneration by producing them as professed original emendations, than by any possible mode of smuggling them into notice. The very circumstance of the corrector's bag having been so indiscriminately emptied before the public (with no infrequent flourish of trumpets as the several articles emerged from it) may prove the sanguine character, but assuredly does not indicate the bad faith of the exhibitor.

PART II.

PROPOSED EMENDATIONS.

HAMLET.

In order to elucidate the principles here propounded and their application, I will adduce a number of passages which have struck me as most likely for that purpose. My chief aim will be to show by examples how incoherence of thought and other allied defects, as already explained, may prove the spuriousness of the text, and at the same time how requisite it is that, in attempting to restore the genuine reading, the conditions already laid down should be observed.

I begin purposely with a passage which is difficult to prove corrupt as well as difficult to amend, and which is familiar to every Englishman; so familiar, indeed, that to disturb it is to dissever some strong associations, and consequently to raise up a spirit of opposition to any emendation which may be suggested.

On this account, as well as to exhibit in some detail the method I pursue, I think it will be expedient both in the present instance and a few other cases, to enter more formally and at greater length into the proofs of corruption and into the grounds for the emendations proposed than it will be needful to do in general. At the same time, I would remark that when I may, according to this last intimation, point out any fault and suggest a correction of it without showing in a full and formal manner that every condition is observed, I am not desirous that the proceeding should be otherwise than rigidly tested by the principles laid down.

The passage in question is the opening of the celebrated soliloquy of Hamlet:

"To be, or not to be; that is the question:—
Whether 'tis nobler in the mind, to suffer
The slings and arrows of outrageous fortune;
Or to take arms against a sea of troubles,
And by opposing, end them?"

Act iii. sc. 1.

Here I am struck at once by a glaring corruption in the text. Not only is there a most incongruous metaphor, from which good sense and good taste have long recoiled, but what is worse, the expressions employed do not contain a consistent meaning. They exhibit, on the contrary, incoherence of thought: what was manifestly in the mind of the author is not brought out: the train of reflection does not takes its natural or logical course:

it begins with proposing one thing and ends with substituting another. The fourth and fifth lines at once fail in proper purpose, and are such in themselves as no clear-headed thinker could have written. How could anyone entitled to be heard have possibly said or sung,

> "Or to take arms against a sea of troubles,
> And by opposing, end them?"

Let us analyse the passage to show this.

Hamlet, oppressed by the cruel position in which he is placed, begins his soliloquy by proposing to himself the question whether he shall continue to live or put an end to his life: — indisputably the plain meaning of "to be, or not to be."

He then proceeds to expand the question; very forcibly amplifying the first branch of the proposed alternative, namely *to be*, into the words "whether 'tis nobler in the mind to suffer the slings and arrows of outrageous fortune;" and we naturally expect him to amplify similarly the second branch *or not to be*, into some corresponding sentence or clause, such as, "or whether 'tis nobler to escape from this multitude of troubles by putting an end to life and them together." In brief, whether 'tis nobler to live or to die by one's own hand. But when, instead of the matter being so presented, the sentence dissolves into something else, a sort of perplexity comes over the reader. He finds the second branch of the alternative converted into "or whether 'tis nobler to take arms against the numerous troubles that beset me and put them down:" which is abruptly starting off from the natural and logical course of the speaker's reflections;—an extraordinary and glaring instance of that inconsequence of thought which a superior writer can hardly fall into.

In short, he first asks "shall I live on or commit suicide?" and then, when he ought to state the same alternative more circumstantially, he proposes a quite different one, namely, "shall I live on, quietly suffering the evils of my lot, or, multitudinous as they are, shall I oppose and vanquish them?"

We may safely conclude that Shakespeare never committed a blunder of so gross a character, especially in a case where it was so easy, I may say indeed so much easier, to be coherent and correct.

That he could not have proposed the last-mentioned alternative is further proved by the sequel.

The subsequent lines all turn on the question whether it is better to live under evil, or die by one's own hand and so escape from it, not whether the evil should be endured or be resisted and overcome. He shows why it is that we submit to the various grievances of life, when it is at any time in our power to rid ourselves of them "with a bare bodkin:" we "rather bear those ills we have, than fly to others that we know not of." Here is not a word about bearing evils in contradistinction to opposing them, but a good deal about bearing known evils in preference to encountering unknown and perhaps greater ones by committing suicide.

The observations which I have now presented to the reader, will be allowed, I think, to establish the conclusion, that the fifth and sixth lines are corrupt; in other words, they are not the lines which Shakespeare wrote.

But it is much easier to establish a strong probability that the text is not genuine, than to suggest with plausibility what the reading ought to be.

After much consideration, trying all sorts of substitutions, and framing numerous hypotheses under the conditions before laid down, I am strongly inclined to regard the following emendation as a near approach at least to the genuine text, if not a complete restoration of it. Let not the reader start off at once at the magnitude of the alteration, but patiently consider the reasons assigned in its favour.

> To be, or not to be—that is the question;
> Whether 'tis nobler in the mind to suffer
> The slings and arrows of outrageous fortune,
> Or to take arms against *the seat* of troubles,
> And by *a poniard* end them?

Trying this emendation by my own canons, I find that in the first place it corrects the gross inconsistency in the train of thought; it maintains the alternative with which the soliloquy began: in the second place it disembarrasses the passage from the monstrous metaphor which is acknowledged by all to be an incoherent deformity. Nor is the emendation at all inferior in tone of thought or force of expression to what it displaces, or to the context in which it is inserted. It does not relax the tension of the soliloquy, notwithstanding its taking away what may be dear to the ears of many a devoted admirer—the sounding phrase *a sea of troubles.*

In the next place, the phraseology introduced resembles expressions employed by Shakespeare in other places. With regard to the word *seat* in the proposed phrase *seat of troubles*, which so used would of course denote the heart or breast, I find in "Twelfth Night" the heart styled "the seat where love is throned." In "Hamlet" the clause occurs "while memory holds a seat in this distracted globe," referring in this case to the head; and we have a similar reference in "Coriolanus"—"the seat of the brain."

Other instances might be adduced to show the familiar use of the term in a manner analogous to that in which it is employed in the proposed emendation. *Seat* is a very frequent word in our author's pages, and is applied in several ways which I shall have hereafter to notice. But the passage which appears to me to lend the greatest support to my emendation, although it does not contain the particular term in question, occurs in "Cymbeline" iii. 4, where Imogen is trying to prevail on

Pisanio to follow the orders of her husband Posthumus to take away her life:

> "Come, fellow, be thou honest;
> Do thou thy master's bidding. When thou seest him,
> A little witness my obedience: look!
> I draw the sword myself: *take it; and hit*
> *The innocent mansion of my love, my heart.*
> Fear not; 'tis empty of all things but *grief:*
> Thy master is not there, who was, indeed,
> The riches of it. Do his bidding; strike!"

I have next to consider the word *poniard*, which it is sufficient for form's sake to show was employed by Shakespeare on more occasions than one.

By the help of Mrs. Cowden Clarke's very valuable "Concordance," I find that he uses this word five times; enough to justify the introduction of it into any proposed emendation, as far as mere phraseology is concerned.

The probability of its having been employed as suggested, rests partly on its accordance with the equivalent phrase *bare bodkin*, which follows a few lines after in the same soliloquy, and clearly indicates the mode of committing suicide predominant in the thoughts of Hamlet, namely, stabbing himself to the heart, not poisoning or drowning himself.

It may be added that the expression *bare bodkin* seems somewhat harsh and abrupt, if it is taken as the first intimation of the particular method of escape from his misery which he was contemplating.

The alteration in the meaning of the passage by

the proposed emendation is doubtless great, as it unavoidably must be, for no small alteration in that respect could redress the incoherence of the thoughts, banish the barbarous metaphor and rectify the want of consecutiveness throughout.

But the verbal alteration by which these defects are removed, and appropriate sense and connexion restored to the soliloquy is in reality small. In the fourth line "the seat" replaces "a sea": in the fifth line "a poniard" replaces "opposing."* Such and no more is the whole extent of the verbal change.

In point of sound the amended lines are so near the received ones, that the substitution of one for the other amidst the various liabilities to mistake prevailing at the time when the plays were first printed, could not have been difficult. An author

* In the progress of the error *a poynard* (so spelt in ed. 1604) might have been originally changed into *opponing*, and afterwards *opponing* have been replaced by *opposing* as the more common form of the verb. That the form *oppone* was occasionally used in that age may be shown by an instance which occurs in Ben Jonson's "Alchemist," Act iii. sc. 2. With these old forms the transition from the text (as I propose to make it) to the received reading would be still easier. Let us put the two lines together.

And by *a poynard* end them.
And by *opponing* end them.

How readily the one would be transmuted into the other is plain. The only difference worth notice is that between *ard* and *ing*, in itself not very formidable.

in the present day, would scarcely be surprised to find such errors in a proof from his printer.

In the course of my ruminations on the passage, I soon became satisfied that I had hit upon the right correction of the fourth line; none that I was able to think of could compete with it in claims to be adopted.

I did not however feel at first equally confident about that of the fifth line. Should the emendation of the fourth be admitted, the subsequent line, it occurred to me, might perhaps be considered allowable as it stood. On reflection, nevertheless, I could not help observing that the line in question would lose something of the little force it possesses, through my emendation of the preceding one, for it would be exceedingly weak to talk of ending the troubles by opposition when what the speaker meant has just been so strongly indicated to be suicide. Beside, in the received reading of the passage, *taking arms against*, which implies attacking, must be considered at the best as but poorly followed up by *opposing*.

Another reading, effected by a very trifling alteration, suggested itself,—the substitution of "*de*posing," for "*op*posing."

> Or to take arms against the seat of troubles,
> And by deposing end them.

One of the commonest significations of the word "seat" in Shakespeare's writings is "throne," as seen in such expressions as "seat of majesty," "heir to England's royal seat," "the crown and seat of France," "the supreme seat, the throne majestical."

In the proposed emendation, then, the seat of troubles might be taken figuratively as "the throne of troubles," and consistently with that metaphor the poet might proceed to speak of deposing them from their throne, the heart, and thus putting an end to their existence. A passage in "King John," might be adduced to countenance this language, where one of the citizens of Angiers speaks of being

> "King'd of our fear, until our fears resolved
> Be by some certain king purged and deposed."
> Act ii. sc. 1.

There would be something in this reading accordant enough with the tendency manifested by Shakespeare and all men of great wit to push their metaphors beyond the first stage of analogy, and it would also be quite consonant with the prevailing humour of Hamlet; but the prolongation of the figure would imply too light a play of fancy for the mental pressure under which the soliloquy was uttered, and would consequently lower the strength of the passage.*

* Besides the argument in the text, it deserves to be noticed that the last suggested reading, as will be manifest on reflection, would scarcely lapse into the received text more easily

On the whole the reading now proposed, "and by a poniard end them," appears to me decidedly preferable to either of the others, and this conclusion is strengthened by some further considerations.

The force of the preceding part of the soliloquy requires that in the fifth line the second branch of the alternative should be stated in plain and direct terms. And this is also equally necessary for the sequel. In the common reading no mention has, up to this point, been made of death, except as it is implied in the phrase *not to be*, and yet the sentence before us is immediately followed by the utterance of the words *to die*, intended evidently to take up the concluding idea of the antecedent clause. Hence that clause ought to speak of death.

In the received text this is not done, as every reader will at once see:

> "Or to take arms against a sea of troubles,
> And by opposing end them. To die—to sleep—
> No more"——

---

than the first; particularly if we compare the several readings when put into the old forms before mentioned.

> And by *opponing* end them.
> And by *deposing* end them.
> And by *a poynard* end them.

And this remark would hold good even if we were to alter *deposing* into *deponing*, although not so conspicuously; *ard* into *ing* is not a greater change than *de* into *opp*.

Here, then, is no proper transition from the conclusion of one sentence to the beginning of the other. The latter does not take up what the former lays down. "To die" has no connection with *opposing*, and to find any kindred expression you are thrown back to the commencement *not to be*.

In the proposed emendation, this defect is wholly removed; the connection is close, the transition natural and direct:

> Or to take arms against *the seat* of troubles,
> And by *a poniard* end them. To die—to sleep—
> No more——

In a word, the expression *to die* so placed requires to be introduced by the mention of the act of suicide immediately before it, and this condition is fulfilled by the suggested alteration, and not by any other of the readings which have had our attention.

In reference to the incongruous metaphor "to take arms against a sea of troubles," it may be observed that it has been defended or palliated by bringing instances in which phrases analogous to "a sea of troubles," have been employed.

Thus, Theobald quotes from Æschylus the expressions "*κακῶν θάλασσα*," and "*κακῶν τρικυμία*."

Shakespeare himself, I may add, has similar phrases:

> "Thus hulling in
> The *wild sea of my conscience*, I did steer
> Towards this remedy."
>
> *Henry VIII.* act ii. sc. 4.

> "Put me to present pain
> Lest this *great sea of joys* rushing upon me
> O'erbear the shores of my mortality,
> And drown me with their sweetness."
>
> *Pericles*, act v. sc. 1.

We find besides, "seas of tears," and "to weep seas," which are rather exaggerations than tropes.

If, however, a thousand examples of such language could be adduced, they would not amount to the slightest justification of the condemned metaphor. The objection is not to the metaphorical designation *a sea of troubles*, but to the figurative absurdity implied in "taking up arms against a sea of troubles," or indeed against any other sea, literal or imaginary. I question whether any instance is to be found of such a fight in the whole compass of English literature, previous to Mrs. Partington's celebrated contention with the Atlantic. The character of her weapon, the only appropriate one that could be wielded in such a contest, is decisive that neither Shakespeare nor Hamlet had in his head a battle with the ocean.

But were the metaphor unexceptionable, the principal proof of the corruption of the passage would, I repeat, remain; namely, that the lines as they stand do not sustain the alternative which in consistency they ought to have carried out, and which it was in fact the purpose of the soliloquy to expatiate upon.

I would further remark that in the passage cited

from "Pericles," Shakespeare shows a consistency in the management of the metaphor there introduced, which in itself, were it needful to urge such a plea in his behalf, would constitute a presumption that he could not have so grossly mismanaged the analogous one in Hamlet's soliloquy. He carries on the figure through three lines without the slightest vacillation or flaw in the imagery—at least till he comes to the very last word, the incongruity of which with the rest strongly indicates a corruption of the text. *Drown with sweetness* is an expression more applicable to a "butt of malmsey,"* than to "the great salt sea."

Hence it may be suspected that the poet wrote something very different. It is the greatness, the rushing, the violence, which Pericles fears will overwhelm him, not the deliciousness of the joy. Our author may possibly have written, nay, I will even venture to say, probably wrote, *surges*, where now we find *sweetness*.

> And drown me with their *surges*.

or better still—

> And drown me with *its surges*.

What strengthens the probability is that Pericles had before made use of the same word:

> "Thou God of this great vast, rebuke these *surges*
> Which wash both heaven and hell."
>
> Act iii. sc. 1.

---

* "Richard III."

It is singular that Dr. Johnson, in his note to Hamlet's soliloquy, totally misses the drift of the commencement, about which I have been occupied. He construes it as follows:—

"Before I can form any rational scheme of action under this pressure of distress, it is necessary to decide whether after our present state we are to be or not to be. That is the question which, as it shall be answered, will determine whether 'tis nobler, and more suitable to the dignity of reason, to suffer the outrages of fortune patiently, or to take arms against them, or by opposing end them, though perhaps with the loss of life."

On this comment, Malone very justly remarks:—

"Dr. Johnson's explication of the first five lines of this passage is surely wrong. Hamlet is not deliberating whether after our present state we are to exist or not, but whether he should continue to live or put an end to his life; as is pointed out by the second and the three following lines, which are manifestly a paraphrase on the first."*

The learned Doctor evidently misapprehends the whole matter: he overlooks the question of suicide altogether, and even supposes possible death from a hostile encounter to have been in Hamlet's contemplation—an oversight and a misconception which, in such a quarter, would suffice alone to indicate some kind of obscurity or confusion not

* Malone's "Shakespeare," vol. ix. p. 286, Boswell's ed.

Shakespearian in the lines that could furnish occasion for them, were such indirect evidence required.

The second passage to which I have to draw the reader's attention is in the same soliloquy, and is indeed in immediate succession to the lines already considered:

"To die—to sleep—
No more;—and, by a sleep, to *say we* end
The heart-ache, and the thousand natural shocks
That flesh is heir to,—'tis a consummation
Devoutly to be wished."

Here it will be seen as soon as it is pointed out that the phrase "to say" expresses a circumstance quite foreign to the train of thought.

As the sentence stands the construction is "to sleep and to say we end by a sleep the heart-ache, and the thousand natural shocks that flesh is heir to, is a consummation devoutly to be wished;" when surely it is not the saying but the ending which is to be desired. Even if we admit the latter part of the sentence, "'tis a consummation," &c. to be an abrupt change in construction, the objection remains: *to say* has nothing to do where it is placed. By simply expunging *say we* every one will be sensible how greatly the passage is improved, and that the introduction of *saying* is a sheer impertinence which could not have proceeded from the clear head of our great dramatist.

The elimination of the two words, nevertheless, although it would be quite sufficient to rid the sentence of an unsightly patch loosely put on by accident or mistake, would leave the metre defective.

Hence there can be no doubt that the couple of little monosyllables in question have usurped the place of a more appropriate verbal combination, to which they must in all likelihood have borne some resemblance in sound or in written character in order to be allowed to appear there.

We have then to look for a word or expression which will strengthen, or at least not weaken the sense, complete the metre, be so far similar in sound or form as to have possibly suggested the erroneous reading we find, and be consonant with Shakespeare's phraseology on other occasions.

Such a word we have, I think, in the adverb *straightway*, inserted in the place of "say we," as follows:—

To die—to sleep—
No more; and by a sleep to straightway end
The heart-ache, &c. &c.

To end instantaneously is more impressive in such a connexion than simply to end, and the word *straightway* not only expresses this but fills up the metre, while it has the further requisite of being frequent in our author's pages.

The similarity in sound between *say we* and *straightway* is certainly not remarkable, but there is sufficient for the foundation of a mistake; and on the supposition that the soliloquy was written out from short-hand notes the word *straightway* might have been abbreviated into *s w*, by any writer who thought he could trust his memory, and afterwards the two letters might have been erroneously taken to stand for *say we.* This explanation cannot of course pretend to accuracy of detail, but is, I believe, substantially correct.

The reasons assigned taken together suffice to raise a reasonable presumption in favour of the proposed alteration in the received reading.

Let us now try the united effect of the suggested emendations in the opening of the soliloquy:

> To be or not to be: that is question ;—
> Whether 'tis nobler in the mind to suffer
> The slings and arrows of outrageous fortune,
> Or to take arms against *the seat* of troubles
> And by *a poniard* end them? To die — to sleep—
> No more; and by a sleep to *straightway* end
> The heart-ache, and the thousand natural shocks
> That flesh is heir to! 'tis a consummation
> Devoutly to be wished."

Here a plain meaning is plainly and fully and strongly expressed. All obscurity and incoherence have vanished.

In looking through this admirable tragedy, I find two other passages both of which will serve to illustrate the principles laid down, and perhaps all the better that they agree in the circumstance of being given differently in the original quartos and in the folios. One of them also (to enliven the discussion) is treated with a third reading in the Perkins folio. The first I quote as it appears in the old quartos, premising that Horatio is describing to Hamlet the ghost of his father as seen by Bernardo and Marcellus:

> "thrice he walk'd
> By their oppress'd and fear-surprisèd eyes,
> Within his truncheon's length; whilst they, *distill'd*
> Almost to jelly with the act of fear,
> Stand dumb, and speak not to him."
>
> *Hamlet*, act i. sc. 2.

The folios all read *bestill'd* instead of *distill'd.*

The old corrector of the Perkins volume substitutes *bechill'd.*

We have then to decide on the merits of three readings, and I do not feel much hesitation in rejecting all of them, on grounds which I proceed to assign.

Distilled is inadmissible, for the reason that jelly is not made by distillation, and consequently there is incongruity of thought in employing the term in the place where it stands. The physical effect attributed to fear is described as accomplished through a process which never produces it.*

* That Shakespeare was acquainted with the various domestic operations of which distillation is one, and therefore not likely to blunder in applying the term, may be gathered from a passage in "Cymbeline:"

> "Hast thou not learn'd me how
> To make perfumes? *distil?* preserve?" Act i. sc. 6.

The other two words are neither of them strictly English, and are not to be found anywhere in Shakespeare.

The first of them—*bestill'd*—is harsh and clumsy, as well as unauthorised by good writers; and I can find no meaning in it consistent with the context. Instead of being bestill'd the frightened spectators are set a trembling.

The second phrase—*bechill'd*—is also unauthorised although not unmeaning, and is never used by our great dramatist. Even the word *chill* (including its paronymes) occurs only three times in his pages, and then as an adjective or present participle.

Let us, nevertheless, examine the grounds on which the correction is maintained by the discoverer of the old folio.

After quoting the passage given above, Mr. Collier proceeds in the following strain of confident assertion:

"All the folios, 1623, 1632, 1664, and 1685, have *bestill'd* for *distill'd;* and it is against both these absurd misrepresentations of Shakespeare's language that the old corrector of the folio 1632 protests. He gives the lines thus, as I am confident they must have stood in Shakespeare's manuscript:

> "Whilst they, bechill'd
> Almost to jelly with the act of fear
> Stand dumb, and speak not to him."

"Surely" (continues Mr. Collier) "no reading can be more natural and proper; jelly is always *bechill'd* or it is not jelly: Bernardo and Marcellus were '*bechill'd* almost to jelly' by their apprehension."*

Now I might possibly have concurred with Mr. Collier in his argument had Bernardo and Marcellus been in a liquid state previous to the apparition of the ghost, but as I am obliged to regard them both as being at that time men of undoubted solidity, I must take the liberty of expressing my dissent from his confident conclusion. *Solids* cannot obviously be *chilled* into gelatine: they can be reduced to such a consistence only by the opposite process of first loosening the coherence of their particles by heat. It is the exclusive privilege of liquids (and liquids only of a certain description) to be *cooled* down into that tremulous substance. Hence the true reading seems to stare us in the face:

> Whilst they, *dissolv'd*
> Almost to jelly with the act of fear
> Stand dumb, and speak not to him.

The intention evidently was to describe, not the cold, but the trepidation, the tremulousness, produced by fright. If this reading required support or elucidation by analogous language we should not have far to search for it. It may be found in

* Preface to "Seven Lectures on Shakespeare and Milton," lxxviii.

an immediately preceding passage of the same scene:

"O! that this too, too solid flesh would melt,
Thaw, and resolve itself into a dew."*

I scarcely need add that the substitution of *distill'd* for *dissolved* was an error of easy occurrence in itself, and quite as easy as substituting it for *bechill'd.*

It may deserve mentioning that when the *chilling* effects of any passion are chiefly in view, it is the blood which is usually described by Shakespeare as the seat of the refrigeration.

Thus in the "Taming of the Shrew" (sc. 2, Ind.) we find:

"For so your doctors hold it very meet,
Seeing too much sadness hath congeal'd your blood."

And in "Hamlet" (act i. sc. 5):

"I could a tale unfold whose lightest word
Would harrow up thy soul, freeze thy young blood"——

Again in "Romeo and Juliet" (act iv. sc. 3), we have—

"I have a faint cold fear thrills through my veins
That almost freezes up the heat of life."

---

* Further examples may be found:

"Look up; behold;
That you in pity may dissolve to dew."
Richard II. act v. sc. 1.

And in Lear:

"I am almost ready to dissolve
Hearing of this." Act v. sc. 3.

This last extract suggests, that if it were needful (which it plainly is not) to find a word ending in *ill'd* as a substitute for *distill'd* or *bestill'd*, a better one might be found in *thrill'd*, or, to coin one after the same fashion, *bethrill'd*, than in *bechill'd;* for it is observable that Shakespeare in several other places describes the operation of passion, especially of fear, by that verb.

Thus in "King John," act v. sc. 2, where the Bastard is boasting to the French that the English king had made them

> "to *thrill* and shake
> Even at the crowing of your nation's cock*,
> Thinking his voice an armed Englishman."

And in "Henry IV." Part I. act ii. sc. 4:

> "Art thou not horribly afraid, doth not thy blood *thrill* at it?"

With the support of these passages, a plausible reading might be made out; although it would be exposed to some of the objections brought against its competitors:

> While they, both *thrill'd*
> Almost to jelly by the act of fear,
> Stand dumb and speak not to him.

Or, if the prefix *be* should be preferred, we might read, "while they *bethrill'd*," which, if not good, would be no worse English than "while they

* The substitution of *crowing* for *crying*, and *cock* for *crow*, in this line, is a capital correction of the Perkins folio.

bechill'd." It will be generally thought, however, if I mistake not, that *dissolv'd* is the genuine reading.

The other passage in the same tragedy also, as I have before stated, calls upon us to arbitrate between two conflicting readings which appear in the old copies. It is a line in which the word *tenable* has been adopted from the old quarto, instead of *treble*, which is the reading of the folio. On the grounds that *tenable* does not carry out the manifest intention of the poet, and not only departs from consistency of thought but is unsupported as an expression by any antecedent or subsequent passage of his dramatic writings, I shall endeavour to show that it ought to be rejected and the rival phrase reinstated in the text.

The passage occurs in Hamlet's injunction to Horatio and his comrades, after they had divulged to him the awful intelligence that they had seen the ghost of his father, and he had announced to them his intention to join them in the watch:

"I will watch to-night.
Perchance 'twill walk again."

Horatio having replied, "I warrant you it will," the prince addresses his friendly informants as follows:—

"If it assume my noble father's person,
I'll speak to it, though hell itself should gape,
And bid me hold my peace. *I pray you all,*
If you have hitherto conceal'd this sight,

> *Let it be treble in your silence still;*
> And whatsoever else shall hap to-night,
> Give it an understanding but no tongue."
>
> Act i. sc. 2.

This is the text of the folio 1623. The old quarto of 1603 has *tenible* instead of *treble*, and that of 1604 has the same with a different spelling, *tenable*:

> Let it be *tenable* in your silence still.

Whatever uncertainty may hang over the text, the intention of the passage which I have put in italics cannot be doubted. Hamlet obviously meant simply to say, "If you have all hitherto kept the matter secret, be all of you silent about it still;" and the question to be decided is, which of the readings fulfils the requisite conditions better than the other.

Although *tenable* has been generally adopted by editors and annotators, and amongst the rest by the corrector of the Perkins folio, I cannot help regarding it as thoroughly objectionable, and as having nothing in its favour but priority of appearance in the earliest editions of the tragedy. My objections to it I will proceed to explain.

First, the phrase *tenable in silence* is scarcely English, from the mere fact that it is never used; and its never being used is evidently the consequence of the further fact, that no ordinary combination of circumstances requires it. It would need some ingenuity to devise a case in which it could be employed with propriety.

Secondly, whether English or not, it does not here express the meaning intended. The injunction which Hamlet designs to convey is that the matter be *held* in silence, not *holdable* in silence, the latter being a common condition of all intelligence, not dependent on any mandate, and which no one in his senses would think of enjoining. The absurdity of such an injunction would be shown by varying the expression. Suppose Hamlet, instead of saying, "Let all of you *hold* it in silence," had said, "Let all of you be *capable of holding* it in silence," we should at once see the inanity of the speech.

Thirdly, the word *tenable* is nowhere to be found in Shakespeare's dramatic writings, although *intenible* occurs once; and singularly enough it is employed in an active sense,—incapable of holding, not incapable of being held*—a use of passive adjectives not uncommon in Shakespeare, and not confined to him.

But, further, the word is exceptionable in this particular passage, not only for the reasons assigned, but also on the ground, not hitherto remarked by any critic, as far as I can learn, that by excluding the right term it would destroy the *point* of the line. A slight consideration of the position of the

* For this remark as to *intenible* I am indebted to Sidney Walker's "Critical Examination of the Text of Shakespeare," vol. i. p. 186.

speaker and of his auditors will suffice to prove the truth of the last assertion, and lead to the conclusion that *treble* is the right word, and peculiarly appropriate in its application. Hamlet is conversing with *three* companions, Horatio, Bernardo, and Marcellus; and, after hearing their joint account of the ghost which was seen by all three of them, he lays upon all three a solemn injunction:

> "I pray you *all*
> If you have hitherto conceal'd this sight
> Let it be *treble* in your silence still."

i.e. let all three of you continue to preserve silence respecting it.

But undoubtedly the word *treble* so placed, although charged with a peculiarly appropriate meaning, sounds somewhat harsh; and hence I am led to suspect that it has been transposed. Shakespeare probably wrote,—

> Let it be in your *treble* silence still.

Let it still continue in the silence of all three of you.

It is easy to see that, when once *treble* had been converted into *tenable*, a transposition would be required; and on the restoration of the genuine text a re-adjustment necessarily follows.*

* And yet *tenable* would be more unobjectionable before *silence* than before *in*, for reasons I have not room to state.

The following strikes me as a singularly analogous expression. Cymbeline (in the play of that name) is pouring forth a torrent of questions to Imogen, as well as to his two newly recovered sons, and their putative father: —

> "Where? how liv'd you?
> And when came you to serve our Roman captive?
> How parted with your brothers? how first met them?
> Why fled you from the court? and whither? These
> And *your three motives* to the battle, with
> I know not how much more, should be demanded."
>
> Act v. sc. 5.

That is to say, *the motives of you three*, not *your motives three in number.*

The passage in the same tragedy which I have next to endeavour to rectify, will evince, like some of the others, how necessary it is to study the course of thought of which it is meant to express a part. It will also exemplify the singular mistakes to which a text printed under the circumstances already described is liable, and elucidate the marvellous ingenuity which, when once such a mistake has been made, is brought to maintain that it is the genuine reading.

The lines in question occur in act v. sc. 2, where the prince is recounting how he frustrated the design of the king against his life.

> "*Hamlet.* Wilt thou know
> The effect of what I wrote?
> *Horatio.* Ay, good my lord.

Hamlet. An earnest conjuration from the king,—
As England was his faithful tributary;
As love between them like the palm might flourish;
As peace should still her wheaten garland wear;
And stand *a comma* 'tween their amities;
And many such like as's of great charge,—
That on the view and know of these contents,
Without debatement further, more or less,
He should the bearers put to sudden death,
Not shriving time allow'd."

The phrase, *a comma*, in the fifth line of the last speech, I should have thought self-evidently corrupt had it not been defended.

It is admitted by all, as far as I know, to be an unprecedented expression. In the only other passage in which the word *comma* is used by Shakespeare, it signifies part of a sentence, a clause, as *period* is employed to denote a whole sentence. In the line now under consideration it can designate literally or figuratively nothing of the kind, nor yet denote a grammatical stop; and to my apprehension it has no meaning whatever. That Peace wearing a garland should stand as a punctuation-mark between persons or abstractions of any kind, is surely as pure nonsense as ever flowed from penman or printer.

The emendation which I have to suggest is,

As peace should still her wheaten garland wear,
And *hold her olive* 'tween their amities.

The poet had before given us the palm and the

wheaten garland; and in the same strain of figurative expression, it is natural that he should complete the flourish by presenting us with the olive, the universal symbol of peace. Thus the proposed emendation corresponds in thought and tone with the context. I scarcely need to quote more than a single passage in support of the mere phraseology of my suggestion. Take the following from "Henry IV." Part II. act iv. sc. 1:—

> "There is not now a rebel's sword unsheath'd;
> But peace puts forth her olive everywhere."
>
> Act i. sc. 5.

Or, better still, a passage in "Twelfth Night," act i. sc. 5, where Viola says:

> "I bring no overture of war, no taxation of homage: I hold the olive in my hand: my words are as full of peace as matter."

But now comes the task of accounting for the transformation of *holds her olive* into *stands a comma*. How could one be possibly changed into the other?

By a very simple blunder. It is clearly (in my apprehension) a case of the incorporation of a marginal direction into the text. The compositor had before him the genuine line, and put it accurately into type, except that he omitted to place the mark of elision (') before *tween*, and the reviser of the proof-sheet, in order to have the defect supplied, directed in the margin that it should be inserted before the truncated preposition, thus:

A comma. And hold her olive ^ tween their amities.

The compositor, mistaking the marginal direction, instead of putting the mark of elision, inserted *a comma* in words before *tween*, under the misconception that those two words were to be substituted for *her olive*, which might have been accidentally blotted or crossed with the pen.

The line would then assume the form,—

And *hold a comma* 'tween their amities.

But *hold a comma* would be so strikingly absurd that he or the reviser of the proof-sheet would be forced to adopt some other verb: *be* might possibly do; but then *be* could hardly have been changed into *hold*, and he must find a verb that at least ends in *d*. Under these difficulties *stand* presents itself, is accepted, and the received text emerges into day,

And *stand a comma* 'tween their amities.

In this hypothetical account of the rise and progress of the blunder, I do not of course pretend to accuracy in detail. The error might have been committed, not in the compositor's room but in the copyist's office, and in several different ways easy to be imagined; but that the whimsical substitution of the alien phrase was substantially brought about in the way described,—that it was the incorporation of a marginal note into the text, I have little doubt, or rather none.

In the 4to edition of "Hamlet," A.D. 1604, the first extant in which the passage appears (for it does not occur in the edition of 1603), there is no elision-mark before *tween*, which is just what my theory requires; for, supposing the error to have been originally made in the first-mentioned edition, it is obvious that the words *a comma* would be introduced into the text *instead* of the elision-mark, and consequently that mark ought not to be found there. But no reason for its absence existing after the blunder had once gained a footing, we find the elision duly noted by its usual symbol in the folio of 1623.

Should the reader, adopting my theory of the mistake, turn to the various remarks of the commentators on the disputed expression, he cannot fail to be greatly amused. Dr. Johnson justifies and explains the received text with so much ingenuity that we regret the waste of intellectual breath while we smile at the bubble which it was expended in blowing. Warburton suggests *a commere*, Hanmer *a cement*, Jackson *a column*, and some one else *commercing*.

Mr. Singer, who enumerates these several failures, adds (after another writer), "I would rather it should be 'stand *an elephant*' than '*a comma*'": and then he tries his own skill with the success (if I may use an antithesis suggested by this colossal object of preference) of the mountain in labour. The *ridiculus mus* in this case is *co-mere* as the equivalent of *common boundary*, or *joint land-mark:*

> And stand a *co-mere* 'tween their amities,—

an emendation which is disposed of by two considerations: first, the word is a compound manufactured for the occasion, and not to be discovered in Shakespeare or elsewhere; secondly, it is difficult to conceive in what sense "peace" could be said to stand as a land-mark at all, especially with a garland on her head; while we may be quite sure that in such a simple passage as this, containing designedly the mere commonplaces of rhetoric, the meaning would not have been left to be hammered out with difficulty, or even to raise a doubt. The genuine reading of this line *must* correspond in obviousness and lucidity with the rest of the "conjuration."

MACBETH.

THE tragedy of "Macbeth" is disfigured by important corruptions, some of them occurring in the finest parts of the dialogue. The first which I purpose to lay before the reader contains a phrase often quoted : I may say, indeed, habitually quoted when it is wished to express the particular notion conveyed by it. If, then, there is anything wrong about it, the call upon the critic to do his best to set it right is more urgent than usual.

Macbeth himself is soliloquising in reference to the contemplated murder of Duncan.

> "I have no spur
> To prick the sides of my intent, but only
> Vaulting ambition, which o'erleaps itself
> And falls on th' other ——"

Here enters Lady Macbeth, and, leaving his sentence unfinished, he addresses her:

> "How now? What news?"

The commentators agree, for the most part, that had he finished the sentence thus abruptly broken off, he must have added the word *side*. Making the whole line—

And falls on th' other side. How now? what news?

Strictly construed, the passage would signify, "I have no spur except ambition;" which, with what follows, would be making ambition first into a spur and then into a horseman: but such a construction, I think, was not for a moment in the intention of the author. He meant, in all probability, the lines to be interpreted as follows: "I have no spur to prick the sides of my intent, but I have vaulting ambition alone which is apt to leap too far and come to the ground."

The term *spur* evidently refers to external incitement, while *ambition* indicates the aspirations of his own spirit. The expression of all this is undoubtedly defective, and shows what I have before pointed out—the occasional imperfect development of his meaning from his propensity to condensation.

On a careful examination of the structure of the passage so interpreted, it will be seen that it consists, not, as at first sight might be supposed, of a prolonged and not altogether congruous metaphor, but, as remarked by Malone, of two metaphors, in both of which the imagery is drawn from the incidents of horsemanship. Macbeth at the outset describes his *intent* as a horse, and complains that he has no spur to prick its sides. This figurative reference to a horse and spurs naturally shapes the subsequent sentiment, leading him on, not indeed to push the metaphor farther, but to express himself in a second allied metaphor, in which ambition replaces Macbeth as the horseman, and is represented as vaulting, or attempting to vault, upon his steed, but from too much eagerness leaping over it and falling on the other side.

Such being the obvious import of the passage, I shall endeavour to show that the phrase, *overleaping itself*, does not carry out the author's intention; that it is an expression inconsistent both with the sense of the context and with common usage; and I am consequently warranted in concluding it not to have proceeded from the pen of Shakespeare.

To substantiate this conclusion, it may be necessary to enter into some grammatical details.

There are two ways in which the word *over* is used in composition with other words as well as by itself, namely, as an adverb, and as a preposition.

When it is used as an adverb it signifies too much or in excess, as in the phrases "he overexerts himself," "he is overestimated," "the horse is overloaded," "the man's temper is over hasty."

When it is used as a preposition in compound words, it has the same meaning as when it stands by itself; or, to express the fact differently, it has the same meaning whether it is prefixed to a verb so as to form one word, or is placed as a separate preposition after the verb.

Thus, to overarch is the same as to arch over, to overflow the same as to flow over, to overleap the same as to leap over. There are, doubtless, some idiomatic irregularities, as I shall hereafter notice, which it might be difficult to bring under this explanation; but, whatever they may be, one point is clear, that, in order to justify their being retained or adopted in a disputed text, they must be shown to have been in common use when the text was written. These grammatical observations being premised, let us proceed to apply them to the passage before us.

The prefix *over* in the word overleap in Macbeth's soliloquy must of necessity be taken either as an adverb or as a preposition; the consideration of idioms apart, there is no *tertium quid.*

If taken as an adverb, the construction of the sentence would be "vaulting ambition leaps itself too much," which is not sense. *Leaps itself* is not English.

If, on the other hand, *over* be taken as a preposition the construction would be "vaulting ambition leaps over itself;" which is equally destitute of meaning. It would be talking of an impossible achievement, such as Lord Castlereagh, some forty or fifty years ago, is said to have slanderously imputed to a brother politician, when he charged the delinquent with turning his back upon himself.

For these reasons I conclude that Shakespeare never wrote, and never could write, *overleaps itself.*

It may be added that in other places he makes use of the same word *overleap* in the sense of leap over, and never in the sense of leaping too much, which is in truth a sense found nowhere, as far as I have been able to investigate, in the English language.

Not going beyond the same tragedy, we find the phrase in question occurring in one of the previous communings of Macbeth with his own dark spirit. After the King Duncan had announced that thenceforth his eldest son should bear the title of the Prince of Cumberland, Macbeth exclaims:

> "The Prince of Cumberland! that is a step
> On which I must fall down, or else o'erleap;
> For in my way it lies."

This instance is in itself conclusive; for I am not aware that there is any example in the English language of the same verb having the prefix *over* joined to it sometimes as an adverb, and sometimes as a preposition.

I have alluded to idiomatic irregularities; and there is certainly one word compounded of *over* and a verb, the employment of which by Shakespeare in the reflected form may appear on a first glance to countenance the common reading which I am endeavouring to set aside. In "Julius Cæsar," Anthony having designedly mentioned the bequest in Cæsar's will in favour of the citizens, artfully checks himself, saying,

"I have o'ershot myself to tell you of it:"

and this employment of the phrase may be found in Sir Thomas More, Hooker, Spenser, and others.

The expression will not bear the test to which I have subjected *overleap* any better than the latter word. It cannot be construed, "I have shot myself too much," nor yet, "I have shot over myself." It must of necessity be taken to mean what it fails to express, "I have shot beyond the mark"—let out more than I intended. It is obviously a very irregular idiom, arising doubtless from the inadvertent transference of a form of speech from legitimate cases to other apparently analogous cases where it violates all rule.

Such irregularities may prevail for a while, and be even adopted by good writers; but they are dropped as language becomes more accurate and precise. Instead of saying a man overshoots himself, we now say that he overshoots the mark.

The occurrence of an irregular idiom in Shakespeare is sufficiently justified if it is sanctioned by custom, and forms no ground for disturbing the received text; but the use of one irregular idiomatic expression is no authority for employing a grammatically analogous phrase in a similar abnormal manner, without any precedent ; and when such a one occurs it justly excites suspicion. Now, not finding any example in the English language of *overleap* being used to signify anything else, even idiomatically, than simply leap over, I am obliged to conclude, that Shakespeare did not employ it otherwise in the instance before us. Besides, even supposing precedents could be found similar to the one for "overshoot myself" in "Julius Cæsar," the subsequent expression, "and falls on the other side," clearly shows that any idiom of the kind must be expelled from Macbeth's soliloquy, and that the text must contain the mention of something on the other side of which there is a possibility of coming to the ground.

The considerations which have been here adduced, appear to me adequate to prove the spuriousness of the text on the two grounds of inconsistent thought and of unprecedented language. And now for the second part of the business. The difficulty of finding a suitable substitute for a condemned phrase, often so formidable, seems in the present instance to vanish, and the path to become easy.

The emendation I have to suggest is a very obvious one, and curiously enough it turns on the same monosyllable which bore so important a part in my proposed alteration of Hamlet's soliloquy. It is merely the change of two letters—the substitution of *seat* for *self*, which entirely removes the solecism in the received text.

> Vaulting ambition which o'erleaps its *seat*,
> And falls on th' other side.

This suggestion is supported, too, by the language of other passages. In "Henry IV." occurs a strikingly favourable line :—

> "I saw young Harry, with his beaver on,
> His cuisses on his thighs, gallantly arm'd,
> Rise from the ground like feather'd Mercury;
> And *vaulted with such ease into his seat*
> As if an angel dropped down from the clouds,
> To turn and wind a fiery Pegasus
> And witch the world with noble horsemanship."
> Part I. act iv. sc. 1.

In "Othello" Iago says:

> "I do suspect the lusty Moor
> Has leap'd into my seat." Act ii. sc. 1.

In "Measure for Measure" we have,—

> "Or whether that the body public be
> A horse whereon the governor doth ride,
> Who, newly in the seat, that it may know
> He can command, lets it straight feel the spur."
> Act i. sc. 3.

Some former annotator, I forget at the moment who, seeing the inadmissibility of *overleaping itself*, proposed the substitution of *selle*, the French for saddle; and it is so plausible an emendation that I at one time accepted it as the genuine reading.

Several passages may be adduced to show that, in Elizabeth's time, *selle* * was in occasional use for

* I adopt this spelling for the sake of distinctness although the final *e* was often omitted.

saddle, as the following from Spenser's "Faerie Queen:"—

> "And turning to that place in which whileare
> He left his lofty steed with golden *selle*
> And goodly gorgeous barbes, him found not there."

It is easy, moreover, to conceive how the word *self* might have been substituted for *selle*. *Sel* is even at this day currently used in the North for *self*, and we know that it was also the case in Shakespeare's days. It is found, for example, in Ben Jonson:

> "They turn round like grindlestones,
> Which they dig out fro' the dells,
> For their bairns' bread, wife, and sells."

The substitution, therefore, of *sell* for *selle*, and then of *self* for *sell*, would have formed a natural sequence of lapses from the original text.

But an insurmountable objection to *selle* for saddle, is that Shakespeare never uses the word; whereas *seat*, while it fulfils every other required condition, is nearly as often applied by him to that part of the furniture of a horse as saddle itself. Little doubt will therefore probably remain as to the reading which ought to be preferred.

I have hitherto been proceeding on the assumption adopted by the generality of the critics that Macbeth's soliloquy on this occasion was interrupted and left incomplete owing to the entrance of his wife. But the passage has been viewed in a different light by Steevens, who, after mentioning that Sir J. Hanmer proposed to read "and falls on the other *side*," goes on to say, "yet they who plead for the admission of this supplement, should consider that the plural of it [sides] but two lines before, had occurred. I, also, who once attempted to justify the omission of this word, ought to have understood that Shakespeare could never mean to describe the agitation of Macbeth's mind by the assistance of a halting verse." He completes the line by reading "And falls *upon* the other," for his strange explanation of which I must refer to his own note.*

Although Steevens's emendation is altogether inadmissible, both his objections are worth consideration. The first is, I think, particularly weighty; and, in turning it over in my mind, a reading occurred to me which would not only obviate both, but rather strengthen than weaken the sense, while the perversion of it into the received words by scribe or compositor presents no difficulty. Instead of "th' other" I propose to read *th' earth*. Let us place the two readings in juxtaposition:—

"I have no spur
To prick the *sides* of my intent, but only
Vaulting ambition, which o'erleaps its seat
And falls on th' other *side*. How now? what news?"

---

* Boswell's "Malone," vol. xi. p. 80.

For the last line I propose to substitute —

And falls on *th' earth.* How now? what news?

in considering which emendation it should be borne in mind that *side* is not in the received text, so that we have to account only for the lapse of *th' earth* into *th' other.* An obvious objection to the proposal is that the line has only eight syllables, and such lines are pronounced by Mr. Walker not to be Shakespearian. In deference to this verdict we might have recourse to Mr. Steevens's expedient of filling up the metre by changing *on* to *upon,* were it not that it would perhaps rather weaken the force of the expression —

And falls *upon the earth.* How now? what news?

On the whole, nevertheless, I think the last emendation is the freest from objection. So amended, I cannot help regarding the line as far more significant, and therefore more Shakespearian, than the one which it would displace. *Falling to the earth* is more expressive for the purpose in view than falling on the other side of the seat coveted by ambition, to which little definite meaning can be attached.

It may seem at first sight that I have bestowed unnecessary labour upon the preceding passage of "Macbeth," when merely to suggest the emendations would have sufficed; and I should have thought so myself, had I not found an inveterate fondness (such as often seems to settle in preference on anomalous expressions,) existing for the phrase *overleaps itself*, and had I not also met with the following note upon it by Mr. Charles Knight: "It has been proposed," he says, "to read instead of '*itself*' '*its sell*'—its saddle. However clever may be the notion, we can scarcely admit the necessity for the change of the original. A person (and vaulting ambition is personified) might be said to overleap himself, as well as to overbalance himself, or overcharge himself, or overlabour himself, or overreach himself. The word 'over' in all these cases is used in the sense of too much."

My preceding explanations are sufficient to show that Mr. Knight is singularly wrong. Of the five words cited by him composed of *over* and a verb, there are only two in which *over* is an adverb, meaning too much; in the rest it is a preposition signifying the same as it does when detached and placed after the verb. To *overleap* is to leap over, to *overbalance* is to balance over, to *overreach* is to reach over. The only strong ground on which *overleaps itself* can be maintained is that it is an idiom; and this can be substantiated in no other way than adducing precedents—for which my own earnest search has been vain.

I now come to the celebrated dialogue between Macbeth and his wife, in which she taunts him with his irresolution, and stimulates him to the meditated assassination of Duncan.

It occurs immediately after the soliloquy we have been engaged upon. Macbeth says to his wife, who has just entered:

> "We will proceed no further in this business:
> He hath honour'd me of late; and I have bought
> Golden opinions from all sorts of people,
> Which would be worn now in their newest gloss,
> Not cast aside so soon.
> *Lady Macbeth.* Was the hope drunk,
> Wherein you *dress'd* yourself? Hath it slept since?
> And wakes it now, to look so green and pale
> At what it *did* so freely? From this time,
> Such I account thy *love.* Art thou afeard
> To be the same in thine own act and valour,
> As thou art in desire?
> * * * * *
> *Macbeth.* Prythee, peace:
> I dare do all that may become a man;
> Who dares do more, is none.
> *Lady Macbeth.* What *beast* was't then,
> That made you break this enterprise to me?
> When you durst do it, then you were a man."
>
> Act i. sc. 7.

In the vigorous lines here quoted there are, it appears to me, four spurious words materially weakening or perverting the sense. I have put them in italics.

The first of these, *dress'd*, is so palpably inappropriate that I wonder it has passed without challenge. Surely it is on the confines, at least, of absurdity to speak of dressing yourself in what may become intoxicated. A simple alteration, a substitution of two letters, restores, I apprehend, the genuine text. Read *bless'd* for *dress'd*, and all is plain and apposite:—

> Was the hope drunk,
> Wherein you *bless'd* yourself?

The expression is quite Shakespearian.

The second word, *did*, seems also inappropriate where it is placed, since with the context it represents hope as looking pale at what had gone by. This would be a new function for hope — a retrospect, instead of a contemplation of the future. To avoid so marked an incongruity, instead of *did* I propose reading *eyed:* —

> And wakes it now, to look so green and pale
> At what it *eyed* so freely?—

at what it had before contemplated without restraint or scruple. It is scarcely necessary to produce proof of the use of this verb by our author. In "Troilus and Cressida," act i. sc. 3, we have—

> "Modest as morning when she coldly *eyes*
> The youthful Phœbus."

Eyed would probably be first corrupted to *dyed;* which would be easily transmuted into *did.*

The third term put in italics, *love*, is a whimsical mistake, although easily made. It is clear that Lady Macbeth is not talking at all about conjugal affection, but about her husband's courage. Love is here quite out of place — a complete interruption of the train of thought. Moreover, there is no propriety in her telling Macbeth that henceforward she will account his love *green* and *pale.*

The emendation I have to suggest is almost sure to startle the reader, but I entertain no doubt that on reflection he will become reconciled to it: —

> From this time
> Such I account thy *liver.*

From *love* to *liver* is no doubt a formidable descent; but let us look at the matter soberly.

The liver in Shakespeare's days was generally considered to be the organ of courage (not entirely to the exclusion of the heart), or rather, perhaps, of cowardice; and a white or pale liver was the synonyme of a craven spirit. Falstaff, who ought to know, tells us that the blood on a certain occasion,

> "left the liver white and pale, which is the badge of pusillanimity and cowardice."
>
> *Henry IV.* Part II. act iv. sc. 3.

Pale-livered, *white-livered*, *lily-livered*, are familiar epithets with our author. For Lady Macbeth to say to her husband, "Henceforth I shall account thy liver green and pale," was much the same thing as it would be for a modern lady to tell her lord that she should in future look upon him as having a faint heart, or (if he had a mane or a mustache), as being,

> "In face a lion, but in heart a deer."

We have changed the organ to which we refer poltroonery—that is all.

The last word italicised, *beast*, has given rise to much controversy. That it is corrupt will be manifest, I think, on a rigorous examination.

The phrase, *What beast was it then?* makes a false transition from what Macbeth had just said. He had declared that it did not become a man to do the contemplated deed, that any one who should do it, would be degraded from the rank of a human being.

Lady Macbeth might with propriety have taken this up in one of two ways; she might have replied, "*What beast were you then* (seeing by your own declaration that you were not a man) when you broke the enterprise to me?" Or she might have said, "Since you say such a deed would sink a man below humanity, what *degradation of your nature* was it that made you divulge your project to your wife?" In the first mode of reply the term *beast* would be preserved, but the construction of the sentence would be changed: in the second, that term would be replaced by another signifying degradation, but the structure of the sentence would remain unaltered. The received reading is a hybrid between the two. It does not ask Macbeth whether he was then a *beast* or what vileness it was that actuated him, but what *beast prompted* his disclosure—which is incoherent and beside the mark, since there is no question of external influence, but one of internal conflict and mutation.

Inasmuch as the first method here described would alter the structure of the sentence, and thereby involve the necessity of several verbal substitutions not easily accounted for, we are driven to the adoption of the second method, which is simpler and requires only such a synonyme for degradation as would be readily transmuted into *beast.* Unless I am greatly mistaken, we may find what we want in the word *baseness*,—

> What *baseness* was't then,
> That made you break the enterprise to me?

By this reading, it will be observed, the metre does not suffer, only *was't* becomes a long or accented syllable, instead of being a short one as it is when the line terminates in the phrase, "What beast was't then?"—in other words, the last foot becomes an amphibrach instead of an iambus.

I will add, for form's sake, that in point of phraseology *baseness* is quite Shakespearian, and it might obviously slide into *beast* without much difficulty.

The Perkins folio, with what it is scarcely harsh to call characteristic infelicity in cases of importance, proposes to read *boast* instead of *beast.* "What *boast* was't then?"

But this emendation has no congruity at all with the context. There is no question of boasting, which is alien both to the character of Macbeth and to the occasion. The question is of daring and manhood. Besides, to speak of a boast making a man divulge an enterprise, carries with it so little meaning that it could not be the language of a clear-headed writer. To make sense would require the phrase to be enlarged into "a boastful spirit."

After this discussion, affecting a dialogue the power of which ought not to be diminished by any error which it is possible to remove, I will bring the passage again before the reader with the suggested emendations:

> *Lady Macbeth.* Was the hope drunk,
> Wherein you *bless'd* yourself? Hath it slept since?
> And wakes it now to look so green and pale
> At what it *eyed* so freely? From this time,
> Such I account thy *liver.* Art thou afeard
> To be the same in thine own act and valour,
> As thou art in desire?
>
> * * * * *
>
> *Macbeth.* Prythee, peace:
> I dare do all that may become a man;
> Who dares do more, is none.
> *Lady Macbeth.* What *baseness* was't then,
> That made you break this enterprise to me?
> When you durst do it, then you were a man.

These slight and simple corrections of blunders easily accounted for, seem to myself to remove four material blemishes that greatly impair the original clearness, precision, force, and beauty of the masterly dialogue in which they have been hitherto permitted to stand.

I will next take a remarkable passage in the same tragedy, which, powerful as it is even in its present state, has been evidently much corrupted, and requires in consequence all the patience and deliberation that can be brought to bear upon it.

It is the celebrated apostrophe of Macbeth to Banco's ghost when the awful apparition had seated itself in his chair:

> "What man dare, I dare;
> Approach thou like the rugged Russian bear,
> The arm'd rhinoceros, or the Hyrcan tiger;
> Take any shape but that, and my firm nerves
> Shall never tremble: or, be alive again,
> And dare me to the desert with thy sword;
> If *trembling I inhabit* then, protest me
> *The baby of a girl.* Hence, horrible shadow!
> Unreal mockery, hence!"
>
> Act iii. sc. 4.

The words italicised strike me as spurious upon the grounds which I proceed to assign.

The participle *trembling*, in the seventh line, is presumably wrong, because the verb *tremble* has been employed just before, namely, in the fifth line; and the repetition of so notable a word at so short an interval amidst an abundant choice of equivalent phrases, would argue a poverty in the author's vocabulary not belonging to it, and weaken the whole speech.

The next expression *I inhabit* (as well as the variety *inhibit thee*) is absolutely devoid of significance where it is placed. Some critics have tried hard to extract a meaning from it, neglecting the consideration that a clear-headed writer like Shakespeare, with a command of the choicest and most forcible terms in the language, could not, in a passionate apostrophe calling for the utmost directness and vigour of diction, have employed phraseology requiring the strained efforts of commentators to give it a feeble and doubtful interpretation. We may conclude with great confidence that he never put those words into that line.

The phrase *the baby of a girl*, equivalent (although this has been disputed) to a girl's baby, I hold also to be spurious for analogous reasons. (1.) Why must it be the baby of a girl, *i.e.* of a *young* woman? What has the age of the mother to do here? (2.) The doubtfulness of the meaning when perfect obviousness of signification is required and is easy to find, proclaims it to be spurious. (3.) Construe it as we will, it cannot express what was evidently in Macbeth's mind. He is asseverating that if he were challenged to mortal fight by a living Banco, and shrank from it with terror as he now quailed before the unearthly spectre in his chair, he would consent to be branded as the most pusillanimous of human beings. Now, with no propriety can either courage or cowardice be attributed to a baby. We speak of its helplessness, imbecility, and want of intelligence, and stigmatise an adult as a baby in understanding; but we do not refer to the little nursling in connexion with qualities not yet developed: we do not call a man a baby in courage. What the text requires is the designation of a class of human beings remarkable for fear, — a type of timidity; and general opinion would doubtless point to young women themselves, not to their infants.

Shakespeare with his own hand has clearly drawn the same distinction in the following passage:

> "The Greeks are strong, and skilful to their strength,
> Fierce to their skill, and to their fierceness valiant;
> But I am weaker than a woman's tear,
> Tamer than sleep, fonder than ignorance,
> Less *valiant than the virgin* in the night,
> And *skilless as unpractis'd infancy*."
>
> *Troilus and Cressida*, act i. sc. 1.

These observations, proceeding on the supposition that the phrase in question means literally a girl's baby, apply with tenfold force to that curious interpretation of it, which represents it as designating a *doll*.* Surely a doll was never adduced by any writer of reputation as a type of cowardice of heart or tremulousness of nerves. The difficulty

* Sidney Walker's comment upon it is remarkable: "The baby of a girl; *i.e. a little girl's doll;* call me a mere puppet, a thing of wood. For *baby* in the sense of *doll*, see Jonson's 'Bartholomew Fair,' *passim*." After citing other authorities he adds, "*Babe* was used only in the sense of *infant: baby* might mean either *infant* or *doll*." "Critical Examination of the Text of Shakespeare," vol. iii. p. 256. Mr. Walker seems not to have had any perception of the incongruity to which this interpretation necessarily leads. If I *tremble* protest me to be a doll, a *thing of wood!*

of replacing the phrases objected to is doubtless great, but that has no tendency to remove the objections to their genuineness. The first of them, *if trembling I inhabit*, might be superseded by *if blenching I evade it*, which comes tolerably near in sound, and makes complete and appropriate sense without any falling off in vigour. Dr. Johnson is said (I do not recollect at the moment where*) to have suggested *evade it*, but without any alteration of the antecedent participle. The word *blenching* is used by Shakespeare on other analogous occasions, and harmonises in signification with the phrase which follows. It does not certainly much resemble *trembling;* but, as I have before explained, where a word is too closely repeated, and is thence inferred to be spurious, the repetition is frequently the result of other causes than resemblance, and consequently the attempt to rectify the mistake does not or needs not proceed on that ground.

Happily for the credit of my emendation, Shakespeare employs the two suggested words elsewhere in a similar connexion.

It is in "Troilus and Cressida," act ii. sc. 2:

> "How may I avoid,
> Although my will distaste what it elected,
> The wife I chose? There can be no *evasion*
> *To blench from this.*"

---

* The suggestion, I find, is quoted as Dr. Johnson's in Beckett's "Shakespeare's Himself again," p. 114. I do not observe it in Boswell's Variorum edition.

As to "blench" alone, we have in "Hamlet," act ii. sc. 2,—

> "I'll tent him to the quick; if he but blench,
> I know my course."

And in the "Winter's Tale," act i. sc. 2,—

> "Would I do this?
> Could man so blench?"

Dr. Johnson defines *blench* to shrink, to start back; and adds, "not used." The word has evidently a close family connexion with *blanch*. It is now replaced by *flinch*.

The greatest difficulty, however, remains to be surmounted in finding out the genuine text which has been displaced by the phrase *the baby of a girl*. And although several readings have occurred to me, they are not supported by reasons strong enough to induce me to venture on the proposal of any of them.

Making the suggested alterations in the seventh line, and leaving *the baby* undisturbed in the arms of its girlish mother, I will bring the latter part of the passage again before the reader:

> Take any shape but that, and my firm nerves
> Shall never tremble; or be alive again,
> And dare me to the desert with thy sword,
> If *blenching I evade it*, then protest me
> The baby of a girl. Hence, horrible shadow!
> Unreal mockery, hence!

The Perkins folio brings forward an emendation of the fourth line here quoted which even Mr. Collier pronounces to be too prosaic:

"If *trembling I exhibit*, then protest me."

It is indeed so prosaic, so flat, so spiritless, where the utmost force of expression is demanded, and would, we may be sure, have been wielded by the author, that it almost suffices of itself to shake all confidence in the old corrector's judgment, and certainly does not tend to confirm the authority claimed for him.

Another celebrated passage in the same tragedy presents us with a further instance of that erroneous repetition of a word in disagreeable proximity to which I have occasion so often to advert. In such cases, since we are usually deprived by the origin of the error of all clue to the right reading afforded by resemblance, we have no resource (I venture to repeat) but studying the relations of things and of ideas, in connexion with the author's habitual modes of thought and expression. Macbeth is here addressing the physician of his wife:

"Canst thou not minister to a mind diseased;
Pluck from the memory a rooted sorrow;
Raze out the written troubles of the brain;
And with some sweet, oblivious antidote,
Cleanse the *stuff'd* bosom of that perilous *stuff*
Which weighs upon the heart?"

That one of the words italicised in the fifth line

is wrong, would be sufficiently manifest from the exceeding distastefulness of such a repetition (how it mars the beauty of an incomparable passage!), were it not proved by the same reasons which show the first of them to be spurious.

The meaning of the word *stuff'd* is incongruous with that of the context.

"Cleanse a stuff'd bosom" does not express a natural sequence of thought. We speak of emptying or relieving of its contents a stuffed receptacle, not of cleansing it *quâ* stuffed.

If we look at the lines immediately preceding the one under present criticism, we shall be struck with the force, terseness, and precision of their language: we shall find every word not only full of vigour, but expressive of some thought perfectly congruous with the meaning of the context. The natural connexion of things and of the ideas which represent them is preserved. Thus a *rooted* sorrow is to be *plucked* from the memory, not *effaced: written* troubles are to be *razed out*, not *eradicated;* or to put the statement in a reverse order, what is to be *plucked* is spoken of as *rooted;* what is to be *razed out* as *written*, and we may be sure that what was to be *cleansed* must have been originally spoken of by Shakespeare as *dirty* or *polluted.*

On these grounds I come to the conclusion that the word "stuff'd" is spurious; and the task remains to find out the term which it has displaced. It is a quest in which we shall probably fail if we are bent on discovering some word, either in sound or in form, similar to the spurious one; but if we look at the natural course of thought and the usage of our great dramatist, the path is plain, and we shall probably succeed. In fact, the thing has already been done to our hands, but unaccountably passed over.

There are, I think, several considerations to show that the right reading is what Steevens long ago unsuccessfully suggested:

> "Cleanse the *foul* bosom of that perilous stuff
> Which weighs upon the heart."

The first and foremost reason, is that the alteration, besides doing away with the sin against good taste, entirely removes the objection of incongruity and want of precision which lies against the old designation. I do not think that the English language affords a happier epithet for the place than the one introduced; and while the term is certainly not lower in tone than the context, it may be literally said to abound in the productions on which we are engaged.

In one place it is used in a way which corresponds so closely with the proposed emendation as to amount to little less than proof in itself. The lines were quoted by Steevens in that view:

> "Give me leave
> To speak my mind, and I will through and through
> *Cleanse the foul body* of the infected world,
> If they will patiently receive my medicine."
> *As You Like It*, act ii. sc. 7.

It is further deserving of remark that these are the only two places in which the poet employs the precise word *cleanse*, and that there are only two passages in which he employs other forms of the same verb. I may as well quote the most apposite of them:

"I have trusted thee, Camillo,
With all the nearest things to my heart, as well
My chamber councils: wherein priest-like thou
Hast cleans'd my bosom: I from thee departed,
Thy penitent reform'd."
Winter's Tale, act i. sc. 2.

Here, again, it is the pollution of guilt from which the bosom is purged. The other passage ("Richard II." act v. sc. 5) is certainly less apposite, if not at first sight somewhat adverse; but, since it speaks of cleansing the eyes from tears, and so speaks (it may be presumed) from their dimming the sight, it is not really discordant with the tenor of my remarks.

I have next to inquire how the proposed emendation conforms to the last of the conditions before laid down, namely, that it should have some affinity in point of sound or literal form to the rejected language (a matter which I have already noticed), or that it should be rendered probable by some other special circumstance. To affinity of the required kind my, or rather Steevens's, proposed amendment cannot of course pretend. There is no similarity in sound or form between *stuff'd* and *foul* (except perhaps the phonic predominance of the letter *f*); but the two special circumstances in the emendation already adverted to weigh greatly and even decisively in its favour, namely, the exactness with which it fits into the vacated place, and the striking conformity of the amended language to that of other plays from the same pen.

My conclusion will, I think, be corroborated by an examination, for which the reader will now be prepared, of the emendation furnished in the Perkins folio. The old corrector allows *stuff'd* to remain unaltered, and changes *stuff* into *grief*:

"Cleanse the stuff'd bosom of the perilous *grief*."

The substitution is unfortunate. *Grief* is certainly one of the last words that I should be inclined to adopt, even if I thought *stuff'd* should be retained and *stuff* abandoned.

Cleanse the bosom of grief (often a perfectly pure passion) is an unusual without being a happy phrase, and, coming after the precise and vigorous language of the preceding lines, must be felt as weak and tame. The chief objection, however, is that the topic of riddance from grief has already been disposed of in the graphic description of plucking from the memory a rooted sorrow; so that, to introduce it again here, would have all the feebleness of a bare and aimless repetition.

The word *stuff*, on the other hand, is vigorous and expressive in connexion with *cleanse*, comprehending in the generality of its signification all that presses so heavily on the doctor's patient, but more particularly shadowing out the remorse to which Macbeth had not before adverted. Those evils about the cure of which he had previously questioned the physician, are mental conditions that might be experienced by an innocent sufferer, namely, disease of the mind, rooted sorrow, troubles of the brain; but, in the fifth line, it is manifest that by the phrase *cleansing the bosom* he darkly hints at what he dares not openly express, the foulness of guilt, the festering load upon the conscience; and this allusion, so necessary to the climax of his interrogatories, would be entirely destroyed by the old corrector's feeble substitution.

I need scarcely mention that the substantive *stuff* is one of those familiar and favourite terms of Shakespeare's, which he is in the habit of setting to perform multifarious duties: thus we find such expressions as "the stuff of conscience" (quite analogous to the phrase at present under discussion); the heart "made of penetrable stuff;" "my household stuff;" "what stuff is this?" referring to what had been said (something in the way of Mr. Burchell's "fudge"*); and numerous other applications of the term.

Another instance of incongruity in an earlier

* In the "Vicar of Wakefield."

part of the same tragedy will not require so long a comment. It occurs in act i. sc. 3. The new-made Thane of Cawdor, absorbed in the dazzling prospects opened to his view by his recent elevation, ends his reverie by exclaiming (according to the received text),—

"Come what come may,
Time and the hour runs through the roughest day;"

which has been defended by numerous examples of similar tautology in various writers, for which I must refer the reader who is desirous of seeing them to Boswell's edition of "Malone," vol. xi. p. 50.

The passage, however, is not merely tautological, but marked by real incongruity of thought. *Time running through a day* may be allowable; but *the hour running through a day*, if it has any meaning, must be regarded as harsh; and both abreast taking part in the race is altogether incoherent. Time and one of its divisions are represented as running through another of its divisions. What Macbeth intended to express was, "Come what may come, time unceasingly goes on through the roughest day, so as to bring it to an end."

We may be sure that Shakespeare would be at no loss to clothe in words so common a sentiment, without affording room for doubt or criticism.

The emendation I have to suggest will probably at the first glance meet with little countenance.

I propose to read:

Come what come may,
Time's *sandy hour* runs through the roughest day.

It will be allowed, I think, that this alteration fully remedies the tautology and the incongruity of ideas in the received text, and it will not be difficult to show that it is Shakespearian both in cast of thought and in style of expression.

In "Henry VI." Part I. act iv. sc. 3, we have —

"For ere the glass that now begins to *run*
Finish the process of his *sandy hour*."

And in the "Merchant of Venice," act i. sc. 1,—

"I should not see the sandy hour-glass run
But I should think of shallows and of flats."

The emendation has also in its favour the facility with which the received reading would have been substituted for it. Mark the similarity between

Time's *sandy* hour

and

Time *and y^e* * hour.

Who can wonder at one being transmuted into the other?

* The form *y^e* for *the* is very old, and has lasted to our own times. Without being able at the moment to assign its date, I may mention as sufficing here that I find it as early as the 16th century in a passage cited by Richardson in his "Dictionary," and I have personally known gentlemen in the present century who habitually employed it.

Being engaged on the text of "Macbeth," I may appropriately mention that I was struck, in turning over the volume of manuscript corrections, with another instance of misplaced commendation, by Mr. Collier, of an attempted amendment in the same tragedy.* He writes: "A very acceptable alteration is made on the same evidence in Lady Macbeth's speech invoking night, just before the entrance of her husband: it is in a word which has occasioned much speculation.

"Come, thick night,
And pall thee in the dunnest smoke of hell,
That my keen knife see not the wound it makes,
Nor Heaven peep through the blanket of the dark,
To cry, 'Hold, hold!'"

After referring to former commentators, Mr. Collier proceeds: "What solution of the difficulty does the old corrector offer? As it seems to us, the substitution he recommends cannot be doubted:—

"Nor Heaven peep through the *blankness* of the dark
To cry, 'Hold, hold!'"

"The scribe misheard the termination of *blankness*, and absurdly wrote 'blanket.'"

The line here in question is, I agree with the critic, evidently corrupt. *Heaven peeping through a blanket* conveys so incongruous an image as to be almost if not altogether ludicrous; and nothing

* "Notes and Emendations," p. 419, 2nd edition.

but long familiarity could reconcile the reader to it, or save the hearer of it from a smile.

But the substitution of *blankness*, although not tending to provoke a smile, scarcely effects a serious amendment. Not to insist on the etymological difficulty that blankness is derived from a root meaning whiteness, rendering it, on a first glance at least, an incompatible term to couple with "the dark," on account of the conflicting associations likely to be awakened,—it is quite at variance with usage to speak of the blankness of a dark night, and equally so to speak of looking through *blankness*, although we hear of persons looking *blank*. No one, I suspect, ever dreamed before of putting these words together.

Shakespeare, besides, never uses "*blank*" in its abstract form. "*Blankness*" is not to be found in his pages.

It is curious that the old corrector, having discarded the long-worn blanket, and substituted for the last syllable of that noun the abstract termination *ness*, making the word *blankness*, did not proceed a step farther, and change the *n* of the first syllable into *c*, in order to meet more fully the requirements of the case. *Blackness* is in every way preferable to *blankness;* and we must bear in mind that *the dark* here is a synonyme for *the night:*

> Nor Heaven peep through the *blackness* of the dark
> To cry, "Hold, hold!"

This reading is supported by a passage in "Antony and Cleopatra," act i. sc. 4:

> "His faults in him seem as the spots of heaven,
> More fiery by night's blackness."

And it may also derive an indirect corroboration from a remarkable expression in the epistle of St. Jude, verse xiii.: "Wandering stars to whom is reserved the blackness of darkness for ever:" in Greek, *ἀστέρες πλανῆται, οἷς ὁ ζόφος τοῦ σκότους εἰς αἰῶνα τετηρῆται.*

ROMEO AND JULIET.

Aт the commencement of the fifth act of "Romeo and Juliet," Romeo is introduced communing with himself in an unusual joyous mood:—

> "If I may trust the flattering *eye* of sleep,
> My dreams presage some joyful news at hand:
> My bosom's lord sits lightly on his throne;
> And all this day, an unaccustom'd spirit
> Lifts me above the ground with cheerful thoughts."
> Act v. sc. 1.

The word in italics is in the earliest edition of the play: the folio reads, "the flattering *truth* of sleep."

We may, by straining, make something like sense out of each of these readings; but they are not happy. Malone supports the first by a quotation from "Richard III.," where the Duke of Clarence is addressing one of the assassins sent to murder him:

> "My friend, I spy some pity in thy looks;
> O! if thine eye be not a flatterer,
> Come thou on my side, and entreat for me."
> Act. i. sc. 4.

But mark what would be required to make the

quotation applicable. We should have to personify sleep, and make Romeo talk of looking into his (Sleep's) eyes and espying there some flattering intelligence, which would be a violent figure; whereas the intention of any one who wrote the line, or adopted the word, must have been to represent Romeo as saying that he himself saw when asleep (or with the eye of sleep) what was grateful to his hopes. It was certainly meant that Romeo looked *with* the eye of sleep, not *into* it. Malone's quotation is consequently beside the mark, and lends the reading favoured by him no support.

The second reading scarcely requires discussing, as it is extremely like a contradiction in terms, and at all events has no special appropriateness.

The Perkins folio abetted by Mr. Collier gives us a third:

> "If I may trust the flattering *death* of sleep,"

an emendation in which there is certainly no life requiring a critical stab to end it.

Mr. Singer, in language exhibiting the triumph of irritability over grammar, says of it: "A more unhappy and absurd conjecture than this of 'the flattering death of sleep' is scarcely to be paralleled even by some of the other doings of the corrector's. I read:—

> "'If I may trust the flattering *soother* sleep,
> My dreams presage some joyful news at hand.'

The similarity of sound," he proceeds, "in recitation, of the words *truth of* and *soother*, may have led to the error; and the poetical beauty of the passage is much heightened by the personification of sleep."*

I should have been half inclined to acquiesce in Mr. Singer's amendment but for two reasons: (1.) It is deficient in special significance. Romeo in the first line does not intend to speak of sleep in its soothing, but in its inciting and prophetic or premonitory office, and thus to connect the clause with what follows, while the word proposed by Mr. Singer has no particular bearing on the subsequent matter. (2.) His amendment sets out from the supposition that the right word must resemble *truth*, whereas, since there are two rival readings in the old copies, we may start with equal chance of success from the other, namely, *eye*. Let us try, then, if we cannot find a term expressive of omens or prognostications, and at the same time readily pervertible into the concise noun which has superseded it.

Such a word, which must of course be a monosyllable, we have in *signs*:—

> If I may trust the flattering *signs* of sleep,
> My dreams presage some joyful news at hand.

I need not enter into any lengthened citations to show that the term here introduced is employed in the sense of omen or prognostication by Shake-

* "The Text of Shakespeare Vindicated," p. 234.

speare, as it is by other English as well as by Latin authors. The following lines will suffice for the purpose:

> "The bay trees in our country are all wither'd,
> And meteors fright the fixed stars of heaven;
> The pale-faced moon looks bloody on the earth,
> And lean-look'd prophets whisper fearful change;
> Rich men look sad, and ruffians dance and leap,
> The one in fear to lose what they enjoy,
> The other to enjoy by rage and war:
> These *signs forerun* the death or fall of kings."
> *Richard II.* act ii. sc. 4.

It is worthy of remark also that *sign* is the only monosyllable in the English language (unless I am greatly deceived) which denotes portent or prognostication; so that if we desire to endue the line in question with this particular meaning, we are compelled to adopt this particular word.

The transition from *signs* to *eye* is certainly not very easy to trace. Probably the first step of error was transforming *signs* into *sigh*, which, taken by any subsequent reviser or corrector in connexion with the context, would be so manifestly wrong as to warrant the substitution of another word; and *eye* being nearest in sound of any monosyllables capable of making sense, it might be caught at, and deemed, on consideration, to be sufficiently appropriate.

CORIOLANUS.

In the tragedy of "Coriolanus" a very simple correetion of an admitted fault effects a great improvement:

> "O, good, but most unwise patricians! why,
> You grave but reckless senators, have you thus
> Given Hydra here to choose an officer,
> That with his peremptory 'shall,' being but
> The horn and noise of the monsters, wants not spirit
> To say, he'll turn your current in a ditch,
> And make your channel his? If he have pow'r,
> Then vail your ignorance; if none, awake
> Your dangerous lenity."
>
> Act iii. sc. 1.

It is unnecessary to discuss the emendations of the Perkins folio, since they have been so effectually set aside by Mr. Singer, who, however, seems to favour the substitution of *revoke* for *awake* in the last line but one. A simpler alteration, it appears to me, will rectify the obvious error with better effect upon the sense:

> If he have power,
> Then vail your ignorance; if none, *awake from*
> Your dangerous lenity.

Lenity is a word characterising the tenour of the policy pursued by the patricians, or their habitual benevolent supineness, from which Coriolanus might very properly call upon them to awake; but, if he had intended to exhort them to any revocation of what they had done, it would have been more appropriate to speak of *acts* of lenity. The sense seems clearly to be, "if this officer has not really the power he assumes, then rouse yourselves from the dangerous remissness which has allowed him to usurp it;" and this sense is brought out by the simple insertion of *from*, without prejudice to the metre.

An attention to the natural course of thought will assist us, if I mistake not, to determine the genuine text of another corrupt line in the same tragedy, which has been the subject of much controversy; and it is deserving, perhaps, of passing remark, that the correct reading (as I think it) turns in this case, as it does in a passage of "Julius Cæsar" to be hereafter cited, on a child's toy.

Aufidius, the leader of the Volscians, is speaking in reference to the Roman general:

> "So our virtues
> Lie in the interpretation of the times;
> And pow'r, unto itself most commendable,
> Hath not a *tomb* so evident as a *chair*,
> To extol what it has done."
>
> Act iv. sc. 7.

The last line but one of this extract appears

to me undiluted nonsense. All the misdirected efforts of the critics have not been able to extract from it a consistent meaning, while the very difficulty of doing it proves the text to be corrupt. If we consider attentively what the speaker intended to say, we shall find it to this effect, that power, when its acts are intrinsically praiseworthy, does not meet with the slightest token of applause from the men of the time for what it has done; and to illustrate his sentiment he gives us, or designs to give us, an instance of something which notoriously makes a very faint demonstration in that way. As neither *a tomb* nor *a chair* can be considered as designating an instrument or medium for the contemporary laudation of meritorious acts of power, our task is to find two words which will denote what those words ought to denote with clearness but do not, and at the same time so far resemble the actual reading as to render probable the substitution of the latter in the place of the former.

The only suggestion with this view, which I have happened to meet with, at all entitled to serious discussion, is the following, which is partly at least due to the Perkins folio:

"Hath not a *tone* so evident as a *cheer*."

There are several strong objections to a reading which at the first glance appears so plausible.

1. *A cheer* cannot with any propriety be called a tone. It may have a tone — *e. g.* it may be

ironical, as the House of Commons knows; but it is not a tone itself.

2. *A cheer*, which must be here construed as a general term meaning the same as cheers, is a loud demonstration of applause, whereas the strain of the passage requires a feeble one to constitute the requisite antithesis between what is merited and what is the least that could be given.

3. *Tone* is a word never used by Shakespeare, and *cheer* is never used by him in the modern sense of shout of approbation.

The reading which I have to propose is as follows:—

> And pow'r, unto itself most commendable,
> Hath not a *trump* so evident as a *child's*
> To extol what it has done.

With our modern associations the word *trump*, which is here the same in signification as *trumpet*, may not at first be consonant with our feelings: the immediate idea presenting itself may be that of the trump of the card-table, with its figurative and slang applications, rather than the trump of fame.* In Shakespeare's pages the term is used solely as the equivalent of trumpet.

My proposed reading, after the first shock has been overcome, will probably be allowed to convert the line into good sense with that antithetical

* "When fame shall in our islands sound her trump."
Troilus and Cressida, act iii. sc. 3.

point and that spice of sarcasm, which are requisite for the force of the passage. The degeneration of *trump* into *tomb* and *child's* into *chair* in the hands of copyists and compositors is easily conceivable; while it exemplifies that insensibility to the meaning of the document before them into which both those classes of imitative manipulators have a perpetual tendency to fall.

There is a verbal error requiring correction in the lines immediately following those last quoted, which, since it has provoked much discussion, I must not pass over without a brief notice. The received reading is universally admitted to be wrong:

> "One fire drives out one fire, one nail one nail,
> Rights by rights *fouler*, strengths by strengths do fail."

The Perkins folio turns *fouler* into *suffer*, which, while tame and rather distant in resemblance, improves the sense. It cannot, however, stand a moment against a forcible reading insisted upon by Malone, which requires a much slighter change and is more appropriate in significance:

> "Rights by rights *founder*, strengths by strengths do fail."

Why this emendation has not been universally adopted it is difficult to say.

JULIUS CÆSAR.

Some of the examples of corruption in the text and its correction already adduced can scarcely have failed to suggest to the reader what a complete transformation of the sense of a whole passage may be effected by the alteration of a word or of a few letters. At the touch of the emendator the old scene melts away like a dissolving view, and is replaced by another which bears little or no relation to its predecessor. Of such a transition perhaps the strongest instance I have yet brought forward is in Hamlet's soliloquy, where the sense of two lines is wholly revolutionised by a few slight verbal changes. As a further illustration of the same point, I may present a simple case where the miscopying or misprinting extends only to a single letter. It occurs in "Julius Cæsar," in the first scene of the third act.

Cæsar himself is speaking to Metellus Cimber:

> "I must prevent thee, Cimber;
> These couchings and these lowly courtesies

> Might fire the blood of ordinary men,
> And turn preordinance and first* decree
> Into the *lane* of children."
>
> Act iii. sc. 1.

Here a reader of lively imagination might possibly picture to himself a *lane* formed of boys and girls, into which "preordinance and first decree," like two pompous officers of the law, are turned, doubtless to march through it. If our supposed vivacious friend should so exercise his fancy, the emendation about to be proposed, simple as it is, would speedily "dissolve the view."

I must premise that the corruption in the last line of the quotation is not (I believe) disputed by any one. There is manifestly no sense in the phrase as it stands. Dr. Johnson conjectured that *lane* had been substituted for *law*, and that we ought to read,

> "Into the *law* of children."

An emendation which appears to have been generally acquiesced in.

Nevertheless it is without force or point, or peculiar appropriateness,—I may say indeed it is even awkward; and on these grounds conclusively not Shakespearian.

If we attend to the sequence of thought natural

* Mr. Craik, in his able volume entitled "The English of Shakespeare," proposes to read *fix'd* instead of *first;* and I think the emendation so happy that I have adopted it.

to the occasion, we shall come to a result altogether different from that so generally adopted.

The speaker evidently intends to say that "pre-ordinance and fix'd decree," or in other words deliberate decision, might, in the common run of men, be changed by such servility as was now exhibited into something notoriously mutable or proverbially unstable — which the law of children (if such a thing can be said to exist, or to be ever thought of) is not.

If he had said, "these servile obeisances might turn the fixed determination of ordinary men into a weathercock, the train of thought would have been felt to take its natural course. Let us try, then, if this cannot be expressed in language conforming to the conditions within which every corrector must move.

The name *weathercock*, although right in import, is plainly too long a word for the metre, and could not by any conceivable possibility have been converted into *lane*, whether by copyist or compositor. It was not, therefore, the original reading; but it has a synonyme which would have served the purpose of the speaker equally well, and which suggests itself for a trial. Let us suppose the poet to have written —

Into the *vane* of children,

and we obtain a reading which chimes in with the context, while it is obviously capable, in the hands of a writer, or compositor, of lapsing with the utmost ease into *lane.**

For the rest, the proposed word is used by Shakespeare in other places with an air of complete familiarity, and as often as its synonyme *weathercock.*

This, it may be said, is all very well, as far as *vane* is concerned; but who ever heard of the *vane of children?* Most people, I apprehend, have seen the thing, although they may not recollect it by that appellation. There is a well-known toy hawked about the streets of most English towns, precisely answering to the designation. In the days of my own childhood it was, I remember, dignified by the title of *windmill*, although it was no mill at all, but only an humble imitation of the sails of that Quixotic giant, easily set in motion by carrying it in the hand against the air. It was doubtless this plaything that Shakespeare had in his mind when he wanted a type of inconstancy implying somewhat of contempt; and the name of *vane* which he here bestows upon it is more appropriate than any other, inasmuch as its sole function is to turn in the wind.

With Mr. Craik's emendation, already noticed, as well as my own, the passage will read thus:

I must prevent thee, Cimber;
These couchings and these lowly courtesies

---

* The substitution of *l* for *v* may have had a mere mechanical origin, from the circumstance that, in the printer's lower case, the compartment containing the former letter adjoins that containing the latter one.

> Might fire the blood of ordinary men,
> And turn preordinance and *fix'd* decree
> Into the *vane* of children.

There arises certainly a slight incongruity from this emendation, which I am bound in fairness to notice and to admit. If it is adopted, Cæsar is made to speak of an ordinance being transformed into a vane, whereas it would properly be the man, the power, the will, whence the ordinance had proceeded, that would be identified with that symbol of instability. Thus in "A Winter's Tale," act ii. sc. 3, Leontes says "I am a feather for each wind that blows." In this, and other instances, the very condensation of meaning which is so remarkable a characteristic of Shakespeare's composition, leads him into inaccuracies which are brought into view when the language is literally construed.

Of this there is a striking instance in the well-known lines,—

> "The sense of death is most in apprehension;
> And the poor beetle that we tread upon
> In corporal sufferance finds a pang as great
> As when a giant dies."
>
> *Measure for Measure*, act iii. sc. 1.

Where the literal construction is that when the poor beetle is trodden upon he finds a pang as great as he experiences when a giant dies; and to avoid this incongruity it would be necessary to expand the last line into —

> As a giant finds when he dies,

to the utter ruin both of the rhythm and of the force of the language. Precisely in the same way arises the discrepancy in the passage immediately before us: the lines —

> And turn preordinance and fix'd decree
> Into the vane of children.

would require for the removal of the defect to be expanded into —

> And turn the ruler who has issued his preordinance
> and fix'd decree
> Into the vane of children,

with the same bad effect on the metre and the strength of expression.

There is another not unplausible mode of correcting the received reading, which suggested itself amongst several others while I was thinking about it, and which is far preferable to "the *law* of children," viz., —

> Into the *play* of children.

That is to say, the lowly courtesies in question might, in some men, turn their deliberate resolutions into child's play. *Play* might have been as easily at least as *law* perverted into *lane*. Taking, however, into view, the superior expressiveness of *vane* with the slighter alteration required for the substitution of the received reading, I feel little doubt that it was the original word. Besides, *child's play* is usually employed to designate what is trifling or easy of accomplishment, not what is variable.

I will just add, relative to the lines quoted from "Measure for Measure" on the feelings of the lower animals, that the defect in construction might be corrected by a simple expedient, well known, I dare avouch, to adepts in composition, and occasionally resorted to by them, namely, throwing the general names which are there singular into the plural number, at some sacrifice, perhaps, of vividness in the effect:

> And the poor beetles that we tread upon
> In corporal sufferance find a pang as great
> As giants when they die.

But on such a ground no one would be justified in tampering with the text, the legitimate aim, as all admit, being to restore, not to improve, the genuine reading.

KING LEAR.

A CORRUPT passage occurs in this tragedy, which has occasioned a good deal of controversy and a number of interpretations in its support as well as of rival suggestions to correct it, none of them marked by any peculiar appropriateness, and consequently leaving the field open to fresh competitors. The lines in question are to be found in "King Lear," act iv. sc. 6. Edgar, after reading Goneril's letter to her paramour, urging upon him the assassination of her husband, exclaims, according to the received text:

> "O, *undistinguish'd space* of woman's will!
> A plot upon her virtuous husband's life;
> And the exchange my brother!"

Malone and Steevens have both unsuccessfully tried to explain the expression in italics. The latter affirms that it plainly signifies *undistinguishing licentiousness:* the former, reasonably enough, demurs to this and adopts Warburton's interpretation, who says it means that the variations of woman's will are so sudden that there is no distinguishable space between them. I cannot conscientiously saddle Shakespeare with either of these lame significations. The old annotator of the Perkins folio makes the matter worse; he seriously proposes, and Mr. Collier as seriously abets,

> "O *unextinguish'd blaze* of woman's will!"

which, but for Mr. Collier's grave verdict, I should have thought could have been received with nothing but that manifestation of merriment to which this long epithet in its potential form is sometimes applied.

We have only, it appears to me, to reflect on what a man in Edgar's position would be likely to say in order to arrive at the right reading. He would naturally fall into the old sarcasm against the unaccountable caprices of the sex: and he would of course touch either on the mutability of women (as Scott did in his celebrated lines*) or

* "O woman, in our hours of ease
Uncertain, coy, and hard to please,
And variable as the shade
By the light quivering aspen made;
When pain and anguish wring the brow,
A ministering angel thou!" *Marmion.*

Perhaps some readers will prefer the Latin *original* of these lines, cited wholly or in part by a sapient critic to prove Scott a plagiarist:

"Femina, quae molles si quando carpimus horas,
Tristis es, et dubia conciliande vice;

on the difficulty of following their motives and movements. The latter was the topic of Edgar's exclamation, into which he appears to have been goaded by the sudden view of the untraceable labyrinth of the female mind, opened by Goneril's letter. A small change in the received text would bring it into accordance with such a sentiment:

> O undistinguish'd *maze* of woman's will!

Maze is a word several times employed by our author. The instance which follows I quote because the passage contains not only that term but the epithet (in a different form) which my emendation would connect with it.

It is in "Midsummer Night's Dream," act ii, sc. 2; Titania loquitur:

> "And the quaint *mazes* in the wanton green
> For lack of tread are *undistinguishable.*"

Although Shakespeare was more likely when he wrote the lines in "Lear" to have in view the maze at Hampton Court than the quaint figures on a village green, and the undistinguishableness referred to is of a different kind in each of the two cases, yet the speech of Titania may be admitted to show at

---

> Quae levior zephyro, tremulaque incertior umbra,
> Quam facit alternis populus alba comis —
> Cum dolor atque supercilio gravis imminet angor,
> Fungeris angelico sola ministerio."
>
> *Arundines Cami*, p. 55.

least an association in the poet's mind of a maze with the quality of not being readily traceable — a consideration which adds some probability, however small, to my proposed emendation.

I scarcely need to point out that it would not be difficult to pervert *maze* into *space*, in the common course of copying or printing. In discussing this passage I have not thought it needful to take into consideration either the reading of the old quartos, namely, *wit* for *will*, nor the suggestions of Mr. Singer in his "Vindication of the Text of Shakespeare." The former has been generally abandoned, and the latter have never been received.

CYMBELINE.

Amongst other passages in the interesting play of "Cymbeline," the following has given rise to much comment:

> "What! are men mad? Hath nature giv'n them eyes
> To see this vaulted arch and the rich *crop*
> Of sea and land,—which can distinguish 'twixt
> The fiery orbs above, and the twinn'd stones,
> Upon the *number'd* beach." Act i. sc. 7.

Crop has been thought corrupt, and Warburton proposed *cope;* but this, as Steevens has remarked, would be mere tautology, since *cope* and *vaulted arch* would here mean the same thing. It would show strange poverty in a singularly rich mind.

Although it is possible to affix a meaning to *crop*, yet it would be a strained and inapposite one, and consequently not to be attributed to our author. I would therefore propose to substitute *prop:* we should thus have in natural sequence or connexion the arch and the support to it.

There is nothing awkward or unusual in this language, as is shown by a line of Pope's:

> "Till the bright mountains *prop* the incumbent sky;"

although I can find nothing in Shakespeare to support it, and accordingly my emendation must rest on its intrinsic propriety, coupled with the facility of substituting *crop* for *prop*.

There has also been some discussion about the second word italicised, *number'd*. It appears to me so abundantly obvious that *number'd* must be wrong (inasmuch as it asserts what is notoriously false) while the negative epithet *unnumber'd* has a peculiar appropriateness, that I will not weary the reader by discussing it further, but refer him to the Variorum edition of Boswell, vol. xiii. p. 46, with the remark that Dr. Johnson strangely professes his inability to understand *twinn'd*, as applied to stones. I am not able to find any other single word which would be so forcible and apposite. The speaker is dwelling on the power of men's discrimination between things apparently alike, such as the stars among themselves and the pebbles on the sea-shore, many of which are as little distinguishable from each other as human twins are.

The corrected passage will stand as follows:

> What! are men mad? Hath nature given them eyes
> To see this vaulted arch and the rich *prop*

> Of sea and land; which can distinguish 'twixt
> The fiery orbs above and the twinn'd stones
> Upon *th' unnumber'd* beach.

Some of the commentators seem to have considered the distinguishing to be between the stars and the pebbles; whereas it is clearly in my apprehension between the several stars and the several pebbles amongst themselves.

In the same play, a rather remarkable compound term is used in the tender and beautiful apostrophe of Arviragus, to the supposed exanimate Fidele:

> "the ruddock would
> With charitable bill (O bill, sore-shaming
> Those rich-left heirs that let their fathers lie
> Without a monument!) bring thee all this;
> Yea and furr'd moss besides, when flow'rs are none,—
> To *winter-ground* thy corse." Act iv. sc. 2.

To *winter-ground* a corse is to me clearly destitute of meaning, notwithstanding some attempted explanations. The sense intended was evidently "to defend or guard the corse from winter."

The Perkins folio proposes *winter-guard*, which is good; but the suggestion I have to offer is, I think, still better, namely, *winter-fend*, which would be as easily convertible into the received text, and seems to me more forcible and beautiful, and more akin in melody to the preceding terms.

It has, too, an analogous compound in another place to support it. In "The Tempest," Ariel says to Prospero, in reply to the question "How fares the King and his followers?"—

> "Just as you left them, sir, all prisoners
> In the lime-grove which *weather-fends* your cell."
> Act v. sc. 1.

Coleridge seems to have been struck with the beauty or the expressiveness of the latter term; for he has adopted it in his celebrated character of Pitt:

"The influencer of his country and his species was a young man, the creature of another's predetermination, sheltered and *weather-fended* from all the elements of experience."

The compound verb which I now propose is quite as forcible and beautiful as the one adopted by Coleridge, and its appropriateness to the place assigned to it cannot be surpassed:

> Yea, and furr'd moss besides, when flow'rs are none,
> To *winter-fend* thy corse.

The interesting play before us contains another misreading, which has been, as far as I can find, unnoticed by former commentators. In the last scene of the last act, Iachimo describes the circumstances which led to his base conduct to Posthumus and Imogen. "Upon a time," he says, "the good Posthumus" was

> "sitting sadly
> Hearing us praise our loves of Italy
> For beauty that made barren the swell'd boast

> Of him that best could speak; for feature laming
> *The shrine of Venus* or straight-pight Minerva,
> Postures beyond brief nature."

Here the phrase in italics wants congruity with the rest of the clause. The poet was clearly intending to contrast the attitude of Venus with the attitude of Minerva, the posture of one statue being well known throughout the civilized world to be bending, that of the other to be upright. The introduction of *shrine*, which has no possible business where it is, upsets this intention at once, and ruins both the contrast and the poetry. In what sense, too, can a shrine be called a posture, and spoken of as one of the postures, or having one of the postures which excel natural attitudes? The alteration of three letters, and the addition of a fourth, effect the restoration both of the proper meaning and of the intended contrast:

> for feature*, laming
> *The shrinking Venus* or straight-pight Minerva,
> Postures beyond brief nature.

My proposed emendation will lose nothing should it recall those lines of Thompson which, according to Mr. Hobhouse (since Lord Broughton), the view of the Venus of Medicis instantly suggests. "The comparison of the object with the description," he adds, "proves the correctness of the portrait."

* There are reasons for changing *feature* into *figure*, for which see Appendix.

The poet (it is almost needless to say) is speaking of Musidora:

"With wild surprise
As if to marble struck, devoid of sense,
A stupid moment motionless she stood.
So stands the statue that enchants the world,
So bending tries to veil the matchless boast,
The mingled beauties of exulting Greece."
The Seasons. (Summer).

There is an epithet used in "Cymbeline" which, although explained and justified by Dr. Johnson and other critics, I cannot help thinking out of place.

Cymbeline, after hearing the disclosures from which he learns the existence of his two sons and daughter, exclaims:

"O rare instinct!
When shall I hear all through? This *fierce* abridgment
Hath to it circumstantial branches, which
Distinction should be rich in."

A *fierce* abridgment is not appropriate to the occasion. Dr. Johnson explains it to signify *vehement, rapid:* whereas the disclosures made by Belarius, immediately before Cymbeline's exclamation, are deliberate, and accompanied by tears of tenderness at the prospect of losing

"Two of the sweet'st companions in the world."

The quotations brought to support the employment of the epithet here, strike me as singularly inappropriate. One is from "Timon of Athens:"

> "O the *fierce* wretchedness that glory brings."

The other is from "Love's Labour Lost:"

> "With all the *fierce* endeavour of your wit."

But surely the very proper expressions of *fierce wretchedness* and *fierce endeavour*, cannot prove the propriety of the expression *fierce abridgment:* they can prove, at the most, that the epithet itself is Shakespearian, not that it is suitably applied here.

What, in fact, is the drift of Cymbeline's speech? It is that the account he has heard of the wonderful events that have befallen his children is too short; it has, of necessity, "circumstantial branches:" and he proceeds to mention a number of details which he longs to know, but for which time and place will not serve.

In consonance with the whole tenour of the context, I propose to read *brief* abridgment, and I do not know that if we had to choose unshackled we could find a better designation. But we are not quite unshackled, since the word wanted must be a monosyllable, be supported, if possible, by similar usage, and be convertible without much difficulty into the corrupt reading. It fortunately happens that Shakespeare has employed the proposed epithet as a prefix to the same noun in "The Rape of Lucrece:"

"This *brief abridgment* of my will I make:"*

which satisfies two of the conditions. With regard to the third; *briefe* (as it would be originally written) and *fierce*, might with ease be visually mistaken for each other, although not auricularly. Without resembling in sound, they are composed of the same letters, with the exception of one consonant.

From all the preceding considerations, I venture to conclude that the genuine reading is *brief* abridgment.

* Boswell's "Malone," vol. xx. p. 174.

THE TEMPEST.

In the beautiful play of "The Tempest" there are several spurious readings, which materially disfigure the passages in which they occur.

The first I have to notice is in act i. sc. 2. Prospero says, according to the received text:

> "there is no *soul*—
> No not so much perdition as an hair—
> Betid to any creature in the vessel."

The plain meaning of which, if literally construed, is "no *soul* has happened to any creature in the vessel," an expression certainly not to be vindicated from the imputation of nonsense.

The common way of averting the imputation is to assume a sudden change in grammatical construction: but there is nothing to call for such a change, no end answered by it. The speech contains plain information, and is not one of those bursts of feeling, or starts of imagination, or manifest turns of policy, or other extraordinary utterances, which alone can justify an abrupt break.

The defect, however, admits of being easily remedied.

Instead of *soul* read *evil*, and all is set right; "There is no *evil* betid to any creature," coincides with our author's language elsewhere. In "Richard III." act i. sc. 2, I find the line:

> "More direful hap betide that hated wretch."

Evil would be written *euill*, admitting of an easy perversion into *soule*, as it was then spelt.

Another misreading of a single monosyllable, not unimportant however to the significance and propriety of the language, is to be found in act ii. sc. 2 of the same drama. Trinculo says:

> "I will here shroud till the *dregs* of the storm be past."

Whoever heard of the *dregs* of a storm? If it meant anything at all, it would imply the mere dribblings of the tempest when its force was fast waning, the opposite of what Trinculo intended to say. He evidently meant that he would take shelter till the fury of the storm had subsided.

Instead of *dregs*, I would suggest *rage*, which it would not be difficult to transmute into the actual reading:

> I will here shroud till the *rage* of the storm be past.

The Perkins folio alters *dregs* to *drench*, which is descending from bad to worse. A *drenching* may be got in a storm certainly enough, but to speak of *the drench of a storm passing*, is not either English or Shakespearian. *Drench*, too, as a noun, is not used by our great dramatist in any other way than to denote (according to Dr. Johnson's definition) "physic for a brute."

A third disputed passage in the same play appears to me to admit of a like simple rectification.

In act iii. sc. 1, Ferdinand, while employed in carrying logs for his hard task-master, says of Miranda, according to the usual reading:

> "My sweet mistress
> Weeps when she sees me work, and says such baseness
> Had ne'er like éxecutor. I *forget:*
> But these sweet thoughts do even refresh my labours,
> Most *busy-less* when I do it."

Here "*I forget*" seems to have nothing to do; and not only is the last line unmeaning, but *busy-less* is an anomalous compound, not found in Shakespeare or elsewhere.

No one, as far as I know, has attempted to supply the idle phrase first mentioned with employment; but several suggestions have been offered in explanation or correction of *busy-less.* One annotator proposes *busy-least*, another *busiest*, and the Perkins folio *busy-blest.* None of these emendations has, I believe, been pronounced satisfactory—except perhaps by the proposers.

In venturing on an additional attempt, I am

bold enough to suggest four alterations, but they are separately small. I would append *all* to *I forget;* substitute *that* for *do* in the next line; put *labours* in the same line, into the singular number; and change *busy-less*, in the fifth line, into *busily*.

The tenour of the passage would then be, "I forget all but these sweet thoughts that even refresh my labour when I most busily do it; or, in other words, when I work the hardest."

So altered, the lines would stand,—

My sweet mistress
Weeps when she sees me work, and says such baseness
Had ne'er like éxecutor. I forgot *all*
But these sweet thoughts *that* ev'n refresh my *labour*
Most *busily* when I do it.

The alterations here made, it will be observed, bind together the parts of a passage before held in rather loose coherence. *Forget*, which in the received text is an idle loiterer, totally isolated and destitute of occupation, is endowed with a comprehensive function by having *all* assigned for its subject. *All* in its turn imparts appropriate significance to *but*, which the commentators, not knowing how to dispose of it, would convert into *and* or *for*. That imperilled conjunction is thus saved from metamorphosis, while *even* connects itself (greatly to the social invigoration of both adverbs) with the subsequent *when*, "even when I do it:" and all these revivified expressions unite in expelling *busiless* and reinstating *busily* in its proper place.

It is scarcely needful to prolong this explanation by adverting to the facility with which the several errors might have been committed, as a mere glance is sufficient to settle that point. I will remark only that the *do*, in the fourth line, was probably caught by the compositor's eye from the same monosyllable in the fifth.

A somewhat prolix controversy has arisen respecting an expression used by Prospero in another scene of "The Tempest." He is addressing Ferdinand, on the occasion of bestowing his daughter on his young friend:

> "If I have too austerely punish'd you,
> Your compensation makes amends; for I
> Have given you here *a thread* of my own life,
> Or that for which I live."

As the third line looks very much like nonsense, some of the commentators have zealously laboured to endow it with a reasonable meaning, and support it by quotations: while others of them maintain that the correct reading is, "*a third* of my own life."

It would be tedious to enter into this controversy, and I must content myself with giving the references below.* It would also be needless; for I think the true text may be determined by considerations to which none of those critics have adverted. If the reader will look attentively at

* Boswell's "Malone," vol. xv. p. 132; and "A Few Words in reply to Mr. Dyce," by Joseph Hunter, p. 4.

the fourth line, he will perceive that the precise import of the preceding expression is there purposely explained; or, what is the same thing, an equivalent expression is furnished for it. Prospero twice describes what he gives: first, as something (say an unknown quantity x) "of his own life," and secondly, as "that for which he lives;" and we have therefore to find a phrase (x) for the third line which will be synonymous with the one in the fourth. In this there is no difficulty. That for which a man lives, must be the end, aim, or object of his life. Let us try the first of these three nouns:

for I
Have given you here *the end* of my own life,
Or that for which I live.

The last line is apparently added by the poet or the speaker, under the apprehension that *the end of life* (a phrase sometimes applied in another manner) might be ambiguous.

The way in which the blunder arose, or may have arisen, becomes at once obvious by merely placing the two readings in juxtaposition:

a thread
the end

After *the end* had been corrupted into *thread*, the article *a* would be requisite to make sense, as well as to fill up the metre, and it seems to have accordingly forced itself into the text.

The emendation now proposed, it will be admitted, raises the passage into precise good sense; and perhaps after this discussion the reader will be more sensible to the absence of that quality in both the received readings. I will first advert to *a third.* What rational interpretation can be put upon a man's saying that in his daughter he gives the third of his own life? and when he follows it up by declaring that by the third of his own life he means *that for which he lives*, we are tempted to ask, what and where are the other two thirds? and why are they not worth living for also?

On turning to the other reading, we obtain somewhat better sense by construing "a thread of his own life" to mean simply one of his offspring; but the language is not Shakespearian, and the only quotation brought forward from an old author that can be considered as lending it support, speaks not of a thread of a man's life, but of a thread of his body, which is not altogether the same thing. Mark, too, the platitude and weakness in which this reading would land us; it would make Prospero utter the tame and not very coherent speech, "I have given you here a child of mine, or that for which I live." Shakespeare doubtless employs occasionally the expression *thread of life*, but always with the definite article, expressed or implied, and always in the common metaphorical sense in which it cannot form, and cannot be spoken of as forming, a gift from one person to another.

Further on in "The Tempest" there is another wrong reading which appears to have escaped the critics in the variorum edition of Boswell, but not the annotator of the Perkins folio. Prospero disclosing himself to the King of Naples, says:

> "Behold, sir King,
> The wronged Duke of Milan, Prospero."
> * * * * *

Alonso answers:

> "Whe'r thou beest he, or no,
> Or some enchanted *trifle* to abuse me,
> As late I have been, I not know."

The word *trifle* can have no proper business here. It has only one meaning in Shakespeare or elsewhere, *i.e.* "a thing of no moment," and Alonso in the first blush of recognition would hardly stigmatise his old enemy to his face as of no importance. What in truth does he design to say? Clearly, "whether thou art in reality Prospero or only a magical apparition of him I do not know."

Several words immediately present themselves, all of them much more adapted to the situation than the actual occupant; but not any one of them comes so near in sound as *rival:*

> Or some enchanted *rival* to abuse me;

i.e. the phantom of my old rival raised up by some device of magic.

We must bear in mind that the King of Naples was Prospero's "inveterate enemy" and had confederated with the treacherous Antonio to expel the rightful duke from Milan. Alonso may therefore with great propriety call Prospero his rival or enemy. We have the two words together in "Midsummer Night's Dream;" Theseus, addressing Demetrius and Lysander, says:

> "I know you are two rival enemies."
> Act iv. sc. 1.

That the king did not consider Prospero as a person of no moment, but as a competitor whom he had injured and whose injuries he was bound to redress, is shown in an after part of his speech:

> "Thy dukedom I resign; and do entreat
> Thou pardon me my wrongs."

The emendation, already alluded to, proposed in the Perkins folio is:

> "Or some enchanted *devil* to abuse me;"

which has so little to recommend it that it may be passed over or left to the tender mercies of Mr. Singer.* If I did not think *rival* the true reading, I should suggest *model.*

I will close this subject by adding that the word *rival* might with great ease be perverted into *trifle* from mere similarity of sound.

* "The Text of Shakespeare Vindicated," p. 3. "Think," says Mr. Singer, "of an *enchanted devil!* This is surely to indulge the *pruritus emendandi* without bounds or consideration for the poet."

THE COMEDY OF ERRORS.

THE next corrupt passage which I shall endeavour to correct, by the light of the same principles, contains a complication of mistakes not easy to deal with. It occurs in the "Comedy of Errors," and is both imperfect and adulterated beyond the necessity of formal proof.

The corrector in the Perkins folio endeavours to amend it by the introduction of a whole line, as well as by the substitution of single words.

In the first part of this attempt he, according to my judgment, completely breaks down.

Adriana, having inquired of Dromio of Syracuse:

"Where is my master, Dromio? is he well?"

Dromio replies:

"No, he's in Tartar limbo worse than hell:
A devil in an everlasting garment hath him,
One whose hard heart is button'd up with steel;
A fiend, a fairy, pitiless and rough;
A wolf, nay worse, a fellow all in buff;
A back-friend, a shoulder-clapper, one that countermands
The passages of alleys, creeks, and narrow lands;

A hound that runs counter, and yet draws dry-foot well,
One that before the judgment carries poor souls to hell."
Act iv. sc. 2.

The Perkins folio corrects the passage as follows, introducing, as will be perceived, a whole line after the third:

"*Adriana.* Where is *thy* master, Dromio? is he well?
Dromio S. No, he's in Tartar limbo, worse than hell;
A devil in an everlasting garment hath him *fell,*
One whose hard heart is button'd up with steel;
Who knows no touch of mercy, cannot feel;
A fiend, *a fury,* pitiless and rough;
A wolf, nay worse, a fellow all in buff;
A back-friend, a shoulder-clapper, one that countermands
The passages *and* alleys, creeks, and narrow lands."

Here several of the emendations are good; namely, *thy master* for *my master* *, *a fury* for *a fairy* (which was proposed by Theobald), and *the passages and alleys* instead of *the passages of alleys.*

On the other hand, *fell* added to the third line, if construed with the verb, is not English. *To have a person fell* is unprecedented, and the epithet is too distant from *devil* to find its home there.

The additional line is not needed, being not only

* This substitution of *thy* for *my* is, nevertheless, not necessary; the wife even now in the North of England frequently speaks of her husband as "my master," and we must recollect that Shakespeare carried the manners and customs and phrases of his own land into foreign countries.

in itself tautological but a weak dilution of *hard heart* in the preceding verse and of *pitiless* in the subsequent one. We may, I think, safely conclude that Shakespeare never wrote it.

Adopting the four emendations already commended, I would suggest the following reading, which I hope every one under whose eye it comes will patiently consider, with the reasons adduced to justify it, before he either condemns or approves:

Adriana. Where is thy master, Dromio? is he well?
Dromio S. No, he's in Tartar limbo worse than hell:
A devil in everlasting *torment laid* him *by the heels;*
One whose hard heart is *batten'd upon seals;*
A fiend, a fury, pitiless and rough;
A wolf, nay worse, a fellow all in buff;
A back-friend, a shoulder-clapper, one that *counter-waits*
The passages and alleys, creeks, and narrow *gates.*

The reasons on which my alterations are founded, I will state with as much brevity as the full explanation of them allows.

Torment is more usually coupled with the epithet *everlasting* than *garment* * is, and at all events, it connects itself more suitably with Dromio's account

* The buff jerkin appears to have been sometimes called, in slang language, an everlasting garment (see Boswell, vol. iv. p. 224), which very circumstance may have led to the substitution of *garment* for *torment.* As the buff dress is introduced with emphasis in the third line below, we may conclude it was not intended to weaken the emphasis and commit tautology by mentioning it here too.

of his master's having been arrested and consigned to Tartarus, a place proverbial for endless torture, where Sisyphus is eternally rolling up his reluctant stone, and the Danaides are perpetually pouring water into vessels that refuse to hold it. *A devil in torment* is to be construed as a devil in the art or practice of tormenting, as in another place ("Twelfth Night," act iii. sc. 4), a man is said to be "a devil in private brawl;" and in the same play (act ii. sc. 5), one of the *dramatis personæ* says to another, "To the gates of Tartarus, thou most excellent devil of wit," meaning an adept in cunning devices.

Laid is rendered necessary instead of *hath* by the adoption of the whole phrase of which it forms a part, and which is introduced to complete the sense left imperfect in that line.

Lay him by the heels was at the date of these plays a common expression for arresting a man. The late Lord Campbell, in his judicious little work entitled "Shakespeare's Legal Acquirements Considered," says (in reference to the phrase "to punish you by the heels" which occurs in "Henry IV." Part. II. act i. sc. 2), "*To lay by the heels* was the technical expression for committing to prison; and I could produce from the Reports various instances of its being so used by distinguished judges from the bench."

We need not, however, go beyond Shakespeare himself to find authority for the expression. In

"Henry VIII." act v. sc. 3, the Lord Chamberlain says:

> "As I live,
> If the king blame me for 't, I'll lay ye all
> By the heels, and suddenly; and on your heads
> Clap round fines for neglect."

Now it was clearly Dromio's design to tell Adriana that his master had been arrested by a sheriff's officer, and he could not have selected a more appropriate phrase than the one suggested, both to complete the defective line in the required sense and to rhyme with the next line when properly rectified. It is in accomplishing both these ends that its special claim to be admitted consists.

The boldest innovation, however, on the received text is the proposed substitution of *batten'd upon seals*, in place of *button'd up with steel*, or, as some have it, *button'd up* in *steel*. In reference to the last expressions, I have to ask, what possible connexion can there be between a hard heart and steel buttons? Why should they be mentioned in conjunction? Shakespeare is in the habit of putting things together with a meaning, with some point or purpose, but in the combination before us there is none. The line is positively puerile. In point of historical fact, too, it does not appear that the buff or leathern jerkin had buttons of steel. In Howe's account of the dresses of that period and of these appendages to them, *steel* buttons are not named*; and in the only place in Shakespeare where jerkins and buttons are mentioned in connexion, the latter are crystal.

By the term *seals* in my emendation, it is of course intended to signify writs with seals upon them, with impressions in fact of the great seal of England†, forming a conspicuous feature in their appearance; and considering the way in which the feelings are hardened and inured to the sight of misery by any occupation the chief business of which is to inflict it, there is a peculiar propriety in describing the heart of the sheriff's officer, whose duty it is to serve the sealed writs and arrest the sufferers, as battening upon the legal instruments by which he lived, and growing hard upon so dry and sorry a diet.

I cannot, it is true, produce a passage from our poet in which the writ *capias* is designated a seal, but there is a similar synecdoche in "Richard II."

* Howe mentions buttons of silk, thread, hair, gold and silver twist, crystal, and those made of the same stuff with the doublets, coats, and jerkins to which they were attached (the latter as being in constant use by the common people); but I can find no mention of *steel* buttons. See Strutt's "Compleat View of the Manners, Customs, &c., of the Ancient Inhabitants of England," vol. iii. p. 91.

† Blackstone, after telling us that the Court of Chancery is the *officina justitiæ*, the shop or mint of justice where all the king's writs are framed, proceeds, "it [*a writ*] is a mandatory letter from the king in parchment, sealed with his great seal and directed to the sheriff of the county."—*Commentaries*, vol. iii. p. 273.

act v. sc. 2. The Duke of York says to his son Aumerle:

> "What *seal* is that that hangs without thy bosom?"

referring not to a signet, but to a written document, a letter, with a seal impressed upon it.

As to the expression *battening*, it is sufficient to adduce in the way of authority, Hamlet's pathetic reproach to his mother,—

> "Could you on this fair mountain leave to feed
> And batten on this moor?" Act iii. sc. 4.

The representation of *battening upon seals* may be supported by analogous descriptions of metaphorical aliment in other places; thus we have in "Julius Cæsar:"

> "A barren-spirited fellow, one that feeds
> On objects, arts, and imitations."

And in the same play "supple knees feed arrogance."*

To complete my argument, I must notice that the corrupt reading (as I deem it) *button'd up with steel*, or *in steel*, would be easily fashioned by a careless copyist out of *batten'd upon seals*.

* Probably some of my readers may with myself be reminded, by these extracts, of those fine stanzas of Lord Byron's on the death of Sir Peter Parker, of which the following noble lines form a part:

> "Time cannot teach forgetfulness
> *While grief's full heart is fed by fame.*"

Whatever objections may be urged against the emendations just proposed and advocated, I do not anticipate a single one against the two next suggestions, the second of which, indeed, follows necessarily upon the first. The couplet —

> "A back-friend, a shoulder-clapper, one that *countermands*
> The passages and alleys, creeks and narrow lands,"

I would turn into —

> A back-friend, a shoulder-clapper, one that *counterwaits*
> The passages and alleys, creeks and narrow *gates*.

Almost every critic has felt that *countermand* was not the right word at the end of the first of these lines, and I am only surprised that the other term which seems to compel reception by its singular appositeness, was left for me to suggest. *Counterwait*, although now obsolete, is in fact the only word in the English language that fits the post here assigned to it. It signifies to *watch against* or to watch with a hostile or counteractive purpose. In the last edition of Nares's "Glossary," it is defined to watch against, with a quotation from Withall's "Dictionarie," edition 1608, namely, "He that his wife will *counterwait* and watch." It is to be found with the same signification in Chaucer.* Shakespeare certainly does not employ

* The Greek verb *ἀντιφυλάσσω* seems to have fundamentally the same meaning. It is defined by Liddell and Scott "to watch in turn," and in Med. "to be on one's guard against,"

the word anywhere else, and consequently its claim to be adopted depends on the singular felicity with which, while it bears sufficient resemblance to the rejected term to account for the mistake, it restores complete sense to the passage and at the same time compels the right reading of the subsequent line.

It is indeed a strong recommendation of *counterwaits* in this place that it rids us of the phrase *narrow lands*, which is an evident and unmeaning corruption, and gives us, in its stead, the good old English expression *narrow gates*, equivalent to narrow ways. I have in my day heard *gates* used for *ways* in the North hundreds of times. Moreover Shakespeare himself employs the word in the same signification, and in one passage, fortunately for the credit of my emendation, uses it in connexion with *alleys*, as is done in the corrected reading of the lines before us. The extract is from "Hamlet:"

> "Swift as quicksilver it courses through
> The natural *gates* and *alleys* of the body."
> Act i. sc. 5.

The next example, although the corrupt reading lies in two words contained in a single line, exhibits four different points worthy of remark: (1)

but the nouns connected with it are explained in a way more obviously agreeable to the derivation; *ἀντιφυλακή*, "a watching against," and *ἀντιφύλαξ*, "a watch posted to observe," both corresponding in import with *counterwait.*

What may be done by attending to the natural course of thought and expression; (2) how totally unconnected in point of resemblance the corrupt reading may be with the genuine one; (3) how, on the other hand, the genuine reading may be perverted by close similarity; (4) how one misreading readily leads to another. I have already referred to the passage in the Introductory Chapter: it occurs, like the last, in the "Comedy of Errors:"

> "Therefore merchánt, I'll limit thee this day
> To seek thy *help* by beneficial *help*.
> Try all the friends thou hast in Ephesus;
> Beg thou or borrow to make up the sum,
> And live: if no, then thou art doomed to die."
>
> Act i. sc. 1.

The commentators have been sorely puzzled with the second line, which every one admits to be spurious. Pope proposes to read *to seek thy life*, but his emendation is at once put out of court by the fact that to seek a man's life is to go about to destroy him.* The Perkins folio suggests *to seek thy hope*, which is flat and pointless; and Mr. Singer, *to seek thy fine*, which is no better, but perhaps more ungainly. Steevens proposes to change the second *help* into *means*, retaining the first — an alteration successful only in drawing down the condemnation of Malone. If we look at what was passing in the mind of the duke, we shall soon

* Steevens on this point aptly cites what Antonio says of Shylock, "He seeks my life."

discover the signification which the line ought to bear. Ægeon having imperilled his life by a breach of the law, could be redeemed from death by no other means than paying a fine of a thousand marks, whereas the whole property of the poor old man saved from the shipwreck amounted to barely a hundred marks. The duke, willing to favour him as far as lies in his power under the inexorable law, says to the culprit, "As thou hast not sufficient money of thy own to pay the fine which must be paid in full to save thee from the extreme penalty of the law, I will give thee this day *that thou mayest endeavour to make up the deficiency by benevolent assistance.*" Now a line is wanted which shall express what is here italicised. We must clearly have a monosyllabic noun in the place of the first *help;* but as in trying after an appropriate substitute all the commentators have failed, may not the *verb* be in fault as well as the noun, and have thus thrown them off the scent? Such, I think, is the case. Let us then try the new track indicated. By the simple elimination of the letter *s*, I propose to turn *seek* into *eek*, equivalent in sound to *eke*, and read,

To *eke* thy [own stock of money] by beneficial help.

And as in those days (before American shops had started up in the world to usurp the name) such a fund was usually or frequently called a *store*, we obtain the line—

To *eke* thy *store* by beneficial help.

which fulfils the requisite conditions and gives us, I have little doubt, Shakespeare's own words.

The language of my emendation is easily supported by quoting corresponding expressions in other places. I will take the word *store* first, and probably a single parallel employment of it in the required sense will suffice.

Where money is concerned I cannot cite a better authority than Shylock. In act i. sc. 3, the Jew says:

> "I am debating of my present *store*,
> And by the near guess of my memory
> I cannot instantly raise up the gross
> Of full three thousand ducats."

Although the verb *eke* is not frequent in Shakespeare, it presents itself several times with all the air of a familiar phrase. It is generally coupled with *out* (to *eke out*), but in one place stands by itself. In the "Merchant of Venice" (act iii. sc. 2), Portia says:

> "I speak too long, but 'tis to piece the time,
> To *eke* it, and to draw it out at length
> To stay you from election."

In "Henry V.," act iii., we have it with the preposition: the Chorus says:

> "Still be kind,
> And *eke out* our performance with your mind."

But for the most apposite passage—singularly apposite in such a case, as showing the combined use of the two words — I am indebted to Spenser. It contains indeed the exact phrase in my proposed emendation, both terms included, and without the preposition:

> "I demt there much to have *ekèd* my *store*."
> *Shepherd's Calender*, September.

Of course an example from another author can be regarded as only a slight and indirect corroboration.

Having said so much in favour of the suggestion, I will again bring the passage before the reader, to enable him to appreciate it when altered accordingly:

> Therefore merchánt, I'll limit thee this day
> To *eke* thy *store* by beneficial help.
> Try all the friends thou hast in Ephesus;
> Beg thou or borrow to make up the sum,
> And live: if no, then thou art doom'd to die.

Thus the proposed emendation not only completely rectifies the erroneous text, but does it in Shakespearian and apposite language, without lowering the tone of the composition; and I think I may conclude that its excellence in these respects is to be received as the crucial circumstance required to determine the genuine reading. I will further remark, how inevitably the blunder of substituting *help* for *store*, which must have been the first committed, led to that of making *eke* into *seek*.

The objection that *store* and *help* bear no resemblance to account for one being transformed into the other, is sufficiently met by referring to what I before stated, and shall hereafter fully explain, that in cases of repetition, resemblance, although sometimes available, is not needed, while to search for it exclusively often misleads.

LOVE'S LABOUR'S LOST.

Most of the emendations which I have proposed, have occurred to me from patiently considering, in the first place, the train or combination of thoughts in the passage under criticism: the one which follows, and which is comparatively unimportant, presented itself from a similar attention to the grammatical structure of the speech given to Biron at the close of the third act of "Love's Labour's Lost."

After having launched forth against Dan Cupid, he continues:—

> "O my little heart!
> And I to be a corporal of his field,
> And wear his colours like a tumbler's hoop!
> *What! I love! I sue! I seek a wife!*
> A woman, that is like a German clock,
> Still a-repairing; ever out of frame;
> And never going aright, being a watch,
> But being watch'd that it may still go right.
> Nay to be perjured, which is worst of all;
> And amongst three, to love the worst of all!"
>
> Act iii. sc. 1.

The line in italics evidently wants a syllable, and the whole question with the critics is how the vacancy shall be supplied. It is something marvellous that in this simple case they should differ. One of them proposes reading "What *I!* I love! I sue," &c. which is plausible, but rejected by Mr. Knight and Mr. Collier; the former considering the metrical defect as an intentional pause. Another editor suggests, "What! *what!* I love!"

Both the readings here mentioned make good the metre, but the structure of the context shows that they scarcely suit the place.

To correspond with the other clauses the line should be:—

> What I *to* love! I sue! I seek a wife!

In the homogeneous exclamations before and after, the particle *to* is inserted, *e. g.*

> "And I *to* be a corporal of his field!" * *
> "Nay *to* be perjured!" * *
> "And amongst three *to* love the worst of all!" * *
> "And I *to* sigh for her, *to* watch for her!"
> "*To* pray for her!"

Surely then it was a matter of course that the line in question should run, "What I *to* love! I sue! I seek a wife!" It would have been going out of the way to write it otherwise, and we may feel quite certain that the little monosyllable was accidentally dropped.

Before quitting this speech, I have to suggest

another alteration of greater magnitude, which perhaps will not be so readily admitted. Immediately following the line,

> "And amongst three to love the worst of all!"

comes the description of the lady: —

> "A *whitely* wanton with a velvet brow,
> With two pitch-balls stuck in her face for eyes."

Whitely (in the old editions spelt *whitly*) has been objected to on the ground that the lady is represented in other places as dark-complexioned. The Perkins folio proposes *witty*, but, as Mr. Singer remarks, *witty* must be wrong, inasmuch as "Biron's whole tirade is disparaging." A cursory glance at the passage confirms this, and shows further that the speaker is engaged in decrying her exterior personal gifts, so that an epithet characterising her mental qualities would be out of place. In the immediately subsequent words, he describes parts of her person by the names of two coarse materials, namely velvet and pitch; and to preserve that sort of consistency which is natural in unaffected speech, the epithet of which *whitely* has usurped the place should denote a substance somewhat analogous in point of coarseness. On these grounds I have little doubt that the received text is wrong, and that the poet wrote,

> A *whitleather* wanton with a velvet brow,
> With two pitch-balls stuck in her face for eyes.

The word *whitleather*, it is true, does not occur at all in Shakespeare, and hence, if it were not found in contemporary writings, we might at once reject it; unless, indeed, the felicity of the amendment should be deemed great enough to over-ride all rule. But we are not driven to this last resource. The word was familiar to those times and continues to be used down to the present day.

Nares in his "Glossary," after defining *whitlether*, "leather made very rough by peculiar dressing," cites the following examples of its use:

> "Thy gerdill made of the *whitlether* whange
> Which thou hast wore God knowes how longe."
> *M.S. Lansd.* 241.

> "As for the wench, I'le not part with her
> Till age has render'd her *whitlether*."
> *Homer, à la Mode*, 1665.

As to contemporary usage it will be sufficient to adduce the authority of Beaumont and Fletcher. In the "Scornful Woman," on Abigail's weeping, the elder Loveless breaks out, "Hast thou so much moisture in thy *whit-leather* hide yet, that thou canst cry?" The author afterwards uses the expression *tawny hide*, in reference to the same attractive specimen of her sex, which removes all difficulty about the absolute whiteness of the material. In regard to the employment of the term in our own day, I can vouch for its being the current name for a kind of leather used in some of our manufacturing districts, and also for the article being of a colour which does not so closely correspond with the appellation or its etymology but that it might be employed to disparage the complexion of even a dark beauty. In other places our author gives us the phrases *inky brows*, *bugle eye-balls*, *cheeks of cream*, *tripe-visaged*, *paper-faced*, so that the epithet *whitleather*, although not used by him, is not without sufficient countenance from analogous expressions in his writings.

The following passage in "Love's Labour's Lost" requires only a single word to rectify it.

Biron, speaking of women in his long, rambling, and redundant oration, says,—

> "They are the books, the arts, the academes,
> That show, contain, and nourish all the world;
> Else none at all in aught proves excellent:
> Then fools you were these women to forswear;
> Or keeping what is sworn you will prove fools.
> For wisdom's sake a word that all men love,
> *Or for love's sake, a word that loves all men,*
> *　　*　　*　　*　　*
> Let us once lose our oaths to find ourselves."
>
> Act iv. sc. 3.

The phrase, *a word that loves all men*, is meaningless, or, at the best, pointless, in a situation that requires point. For the suggestions and remarks to which it has given rise I must refer to Boswell's Variorum edition, vol. iv. p. 390. A brief attention to the course of thought will I think yield the true reading. A comparison is made between wisdom and love — the wisdom which men love is placed in a sort of antithesis with the love which does something to men — the received text says which *loves* men, but the parallel evidently requires the sense to be "which gives wisdom to all men." The change of a few letters effects this as follows: —

> For wisdom's sake a word that all men love,
> Or for love's sake, a word that *learns* all men,

in the sense of *teaches* all men, which is what Biron has been so long harping upon. I may add that a plausible reading would be obtained by a transposition of the concluding phrase, making it "a word that *all men learn*," but it would be at the expense of the antithesis.

In a subsequent part of the drama before us, another error occurs: Rosaline says,

> "So *pertaunt-like* would I o'ersway his state,
> That he should be my fool and I his fate."
>
> Act v. sc. 2.

Portent-like say the commentators: *potently* says the Perkins folio, with much more plausibility.

The latter reading, it is fair to say, is countenanced by a passage in "Coriolanus," Act ii. sc. 3. Brutus, speaking of Coriolanus to the people, says that he

> "Ever spake against
> Your liberties and the charters that you bear
> I'th body of the weal: and now, arriving
> A place of *potency* and *sway of the state*," &c. &c.

There is a compound adverb, however, which seems to fill the place of the unprecedented phrase that has been expelled, more happily than either of the proposed emendations, namely, *potentate-like:* "she would rule his state like a monarch." The first part of the word must of course be pronounced as a dissyllable:

> So *pot'ntate-like* would I o'ersway his state,
> That he should be my fool and I his fate.

The term *potentate* is used again in the same scene,

> "Dost thou infamonize me among *potentates?*"

A MIDSUMMER-NIGHT'S DREAM.

In this admirable drama an extraordinary blunder has established itself in the text.

Demetrius, on awakening from a supernatural sleep, bursts forth into extravagant praises of Helena; and lavishes the following hyperbolical eulogium on the whiteness of her hand. He says to her, —

> "That pure congealèd white, high Taurus' snow,
> Fann'd with the eastern wind, turns to a crow,
> When thou hold'st up thy hand: O let me kiss
> *This princess of pure white*, this seal of bliss!
> Act iii. sc. 2.

The expression in italics is (to me at least) obviously corrupt, and has naturally enough perplexed some of the critics. Sir Thomas Hanmer reads *this pureness of pure white*, which is adopted by Dr. Warburton, but does not commend itself by any special appositeness. Steevens and Malone support the old reading by citing such expressions as the "princess of fruits," applied by Sir Walter Raleigh to the pine-apple, and "the queen of curds and cream," applied in the "Winter's Tale" to Perdita, both of which appear to me irrelevant. The Perkins folio, backed without scruple by Mr. Collier, gives us "the impress of pure white," of which I can make no sense.

In reference to the two quotations, adduced by Steevens and Malone to support the received text, it deserves to be remarked that the titles of dignity therein severally mentioned are used in two different ways, and could not consequently *both* be applicable. *The pine-apple* in the first is placed at the head of its own class, denominated *fruits;* while, in the second quotation, *curds and cream* do not, I take it, form a class of which Perdita is the head, but constitute the territory over which she reigns; yet Malone cites the second passage as confirming the received text like the first. *The princess of pure white* cannot, if I am correct, avail herself of both offers to support her.

Since the proposed readings are none of them quite satisfactory, I will suggest another, which has occurred to me from looking to the tenour of the passage. Demetrius evidently wishes to extol the whiteness of Helena's hand as reaching the utmost perfection. I therefore propose to read,

This *quintessence of white,* this seal of bliss.

It is an emendation which at any rate must be allowed to make good sense of the line, without straining on the one hand or refining on the other.

The accent must, of course, be on the first syllable, as it is in the passage I am going to cite in support of my proposal from "As You Like It," act iii. sc. 2:

> "The quintessence of every sprite
> Heaven would in little show."

I have still two points to account for, the introduction of *pure* before *white*, and the transmutation of *quintessence* into *princess.* The latter is such a blunder as almost any printing-office might turn out. Inasmuch as the two main sounds in each of the words (*in* and *ess*) correspond, one of the terms would be easily converted into the other, and when once *quintessence* had been changed into *princess*, the addition of *pure* would naturally follow in order to complete the metre.

After this explanation, let me bring the passage before the reader again, and he will probably acquiesce in the appropriateness of the emendation.

> That pure congealèd white, high Taurus' snow,
> Fann'd with the eastern wind, turns to a crow,
> When thou hold'st up thy hand: O let me kiss
> This *quintessence* of white, this seal of bliss!

Since writing the above, I have recollected another passage in Shakespeare which still better supports my proposed amendment, than the quotation from "As You Like It," and will at all events serve as a corroboration.

The same remarkable term on which the emendation turns, is made use of by Hamlet in his celebrated exclamation on the nature of his own species: "What a piece of work is man! How noble in reason! how infinite in faculty! in form, and moving, how express and admirable! In action how like an angel! in apprehension how like a god! the beauty of the world! The paragon of animals! And yet to me what is *this quinessence of dust?*"*

* Hamlet, act ii. sc. 2.

THE MERCHANT OF VENICE.

THAT delightful comedy the "Merchant of Venice," furnishes several instances of errors in copying or printing.

In act i. sc. 3, there is a verbal repetition, which, although it does not injure the sense, is displeasing, and might be easily removed. Antonio says to his friend, in reference to Shylock's appeal to the patriarch Jacob,

> "An evil soul, producing holy witness,
> Is like a villain with a smiling cheek;
> A *goodly* apple rotten at the heart;
> O, what a *goodly* outside falsehood hath!"

I suggest *comely* in place of the second *goodly*,

> O, what a *comely* outside falsehood hath!

To support the emendation, I will adduce only one quotation from our author:

> "O what a world is this when what is *comely*
> Envenoms him that bears it!"
>
> *As You Like It.*

The use of the two words in those days, and

their wont to go in couples, are well shown by a passage in "Ascham's Schoolmaster," describing what kind of being 'Ευφυης is. Amongst other things he has "a countenance not werish and crabbed, but fair and *comely;* a personage not wretched and deformed, but tall and *goodly;* for surely a *comely* countenance with a *goodly* stature, giveth credit to learning, and authority to the person." Afterwards he speaks of a *comely* personage, and a *comely* body. Mr. Sidney Walker* suggests *godly* in place of the second *goodly*, and shows by numerous citations how frequently *good* and *god* are misprinted for each other. His emendation, nevertheless, appears to me more displeasing from the very nearness of the sound than the old reading from its identity.

The same play (act iii. sc. 1) presents us with a remarkable instance in which even the partial repetition of a word is generally, and I think justly, regarded as a proof of corruption:

> "Thus ornament is but the guilèd shore
> To a most dangerous sea; the *beauteous* scarf
> Veiling an *Indian beauty;* in a word,
> The seeming truth which cunning times put on
> To entrap the wisest."

The greatest defect here, however, is not the repetition (although that is great enough), but it is that the intention of the poet is evidently de-

* "Critical Examination of the Text of Shakespeare," vol. i. p. 303.

feated. He meant his beauteous scarf to veil something *not* beautiful: otherwise the point would be lost. Now of those things which a scarf is capable of covering, or usually employed to cover, what is most unsightly to us in an Indian may be said to be his colour, and I would accordingly propose to read,

Veiling an *Indian's blackness,*

which expresses in the most direct way, what was manifestly in the author's mind. In former times the colour was certainly not regarded with greater favour than it is at present. It is said in Barclay's "Ship of Fooles":

"He that goeth right, steadfast, sure, and fast,
May well him mocke that goeth halting and lame,
And he that is *white* may well his scornes cast,
Agaynst a man of Inde."

I ought perhaps to notice the amendments of Sir Thomas Hanmer, and of the Perkins folio; but they are both so unlikely that I must content myself with merely referring to them.

The same play in the second scene of the third act, presents us with an unquestionable error, which the critics have altogether failed to set right.

Referring to Portia's portrait and the painter of it, Bassanio exclaims:

"But her eyes,—
How could he see to do them? Having made one,
Methinks, it should have pow'r to steal both his,
And leave itself *unfurnish'd.*"

For the explanation and defence of the last word which has really no appropriateness, and scarcely an assignable meaning where it is placed, I must refer to the Variorum edition of 1821, vol. v. p. 86. The vindication of the received text strikes me as wholly unsuccessful. To speak of one eye in the portrait leaving itself (by having destroyed the sight of the painter) *unfurnished*, seems exceedingly vague if not entirely destitute of sense; and the phrase could scarcely have proceeded from any writer who had a passable command of language. However it may be interpreted, it does not give the natural sequel of the preceding sentiments, which, fantastical as they are, almost beyond a lover's licence, must be consistent amongst themselves.

Fortunately there is a word used by Shakespeare in another place which so exactly expresses what he evidently meant to say here, and might be so readily transformed into the received reading, that I have little doubt it was the epithet which *unfurnished* has "pushed from its stool." It is *unfellowed*,

> And leave itself *unfellow'd.*

Osric says to Hamlet, speaking in commendation of Laertes,

> "In his meed, he is *unfellowed.*"—Act v. sc. 2.

If I mistake not, to name this emendation is to ensure its reception.

AS YOU LIKE IT.

There is a passage in this drama overlooked by the commentators in the Variorum edition of Boswell and Malone, but which appears to me corrupt on the ground of containing a tasteless, and even disagreeable repetition, and which, on account of its excellence in other respects, it is desirable should be freed from all blemish. Orlando says to Adam, an old serving-man: —

> "O, good old man; how well in thee appears
> The constant *service* of the antique world,
> Where *service* sweat for duty not for meed!"
>
> Act ii. sc. 3.

Mr. Walker remarks, that it is the first *service* which in his opinion is corrupt, yet he can imagine (he continues,) Shakespeare to have written,

> "Where *duty* sweat for duty not for meed,"

which to my taste would spoil the line. There is no reason why *duty* should be repeated, and if so, the repetition must weaken the sentiment. The

Perkins folio presents us with *favour* instead of the first *service*, but it is feeble, and has no appositeness or superiority in any way over several other words which might be inserted. I propose to read *fealty* as follows:

> O, good old man! how well in thee appears
> The constant *fealty* of the antique world,
> Where service sweat for duty, not for meed!

I know no word in the English language which so happily fits the context, and Shakespeare, in another place, couples the quality in question with the attribute of durableness.

> "I am in parliament pledge for his truth,
> And *lasting fealty* to the new-made king."
>
> *Richard II.* act v. sc. 2.

PART III.

INDETERMINATE READINGS.

A GREAT number of passages which have been corrupted in various ways must, as I have before remarked, remain, after all is done, in a dubious position. Each of them admits of being corrected in several different modes equally plausible. Not any of the emendations proposed exhibits a marked superiority over the rest.

In these cases it is often useful, and sometimes necessary, to examine the claims of the suggested readings and to put the result on record.

Considerations may occur to future inquirers, upon a review of them, which will determine the superiority amongst competitors at present apparently equal, or bring a new one into the field which will unite all voices in its favour. And even should no advantage of this sort accrue, it is frequently indispensable to scrutinise and invalidate proposals urged, perhaps with undoubting confidence, and even incorporated into the text of current editions, although you may have no unquestionable emendation to bring forward yourself, and can only show that the reading is to be held as doubtful, and waiting for any new light that may be cast upon it. With these aims I proceed, in the present section, to discuss a number of instances in which the described indeterminateness exists, and cannot with our actual resources be dispelled.

CORIOLANUS.

THE tragedy of "Coriolanus," as we have already had occasion to notice, contains numerous corruptions, and it furnishes several examples of doubtful readings.

Amongst these, the one I am about to adduce has caused considerable controversy. Coriolanus himself is speaking:

> "Therefore, beseech you,—
> You that will be less fearful than discreet;
> That love the fundamental part of state
> More than you doubt the change on't; that prefer
> A noble life before a long, and wish
> To *jump* a body with a dangerous physic
> That's sure of death without it,—at once pluck out
> The multitudinous tongue." Act iii. sc. 1.

To jump, in this connection, although supported by Steevens and Malone, has been, whether justly or not, discarded by several modern editors and annotators. The expression adduced by the former, in reference to hellebore, "it putteth a body to a jump or great hazard," is not precisely the same phraseology as the expression *to jump a body*, for which there is not any plausible precedent to be found in Shakespeare, and it would in this place be, at the best, a somewhat awkward term.

Jump, nevertheless, is preferable both to Mr. Singer's *imp*, and to a reading noticed by Steevens —*vamp*.

To *vamp* a body would signify to patch or piece it, which is not here in question, and this is also the meaning ingeniously extracted by Mr. Singer from *imp*.

The speaker manifestly intends to say to his audience, in substance, "you that have nerve enough to make trial of a dangerous medicine, which may cure the body, and at the worst will only result in that death which is sure to take place without it, at once pluck out," &c., &c.

Now, if we discard *jump*, we want a word in its place which will help to express this, and not differ from it too much in point of sound. Of all the terms I can think of, *tempt* is the one that accomplishes the desired end the best:

> To tempt a body with a dangerous physic
> That's sure of death without it.

i. e. to *try* a body, to make an experiment upon it. So in "Henry VIII.," act i. sc. 2, we have

> "I am much too venturous
> In *tempting* of your patience."

I scarcely need point out how well this sense agrees with the Latin etymon of the verb *tento, tentare*, of which the radical and paramount signification is *to try;* and the word is to be found with the same import in our early English writers as well as in the current literature of the day.

In Wickliffe's translation of the Bible there is a good example to the purpose: "I beseech tempt or assaie (tenta) vs thi seruauntis ten days" (Dan. i. 12); which passage is rendered in the authorised version, "Prove thy servants, I beseech thee, ten days." Here, I think, are ample grounds for accounting the text doubtful, but if the question were required to be imperatively decided, I should be disposed to give my voice in favour of the received reading.

Under the head of indeterminate readings, may be ranked many of those which have been dealt with by the old corrector in the Perkins folio. As an example, I will take a passage in the same tragedy of "Coriolanus." Volumnia is addressing her exasperated son:

> "Pray be counsell'd.
> I have a heart as little *apt* as yours,
> But yet a brain that leads my use of anger
> To better vantage." Act iii. sc. 2.

To remedy the obvious solecism here, the Perkins folio introduces a whole line:*

* Collier's "Notes and Emendations," p. 361, 2nd edition.

"I have a heart as little apt as yours
To brook control without the use of anger,
But yet a brain that leads my use of anger
To better vantage."

This interpolation undoubtedly restores sense to the prior line, but there is no external evidence for it; there are no grounds for admitting it in preference to a score of other amendments; and it does not commend itself to our acceptance by any peculiar felicity. Although I cannot unite with Mr. Singer in calling it absurd, I agree with him that "if a line is missing it must have been something very different."*

Far from being happy, the new line is indeed intrinsically feeble, while it causes an awkward repetition of the phrase "use of anger," and if I mistake not, involves the necessity of putting a different construction on the repeated phrase in each line,— confounds, in fact, two different meanings. In the interpolated line *the use of anger* can mean only *actual anger:* in the next line it means *proneness* to anger — the custom or habit of growing angry. Other lines, moreover, by the score, might be devised that would answer the purpose equally well; *e.g.*

To bear unmov'd the people's rude demands.

But without the violence of interpolating a line for which no evidence can be brought, due signi-

* "The Text of Shakespeare Vindicated," p. 220.

ficance may be given to the passage by substituting a single word. Let "*apt*" be replaced by "*cool*," or "*calm*," or "*tame*:"

> I have a heart as little *cool* as yours,
> But yet a brain that leads my use of anger
> To better vantage.

The proposed substitution would, at all events, effect the requisite antithesis between the fiery heart and the cool head. Mr. Singer suggests *soft*, which perhaps would more easily slide into the received reading than any other epithet; but a *heart* may be hard without being irritable, and the latter attribute seems to be required by the context.

Another mode of dealing with the faulty line also suggests itself. Allowing "apt," which is rather a sounding word, to stand as it is, let us try the effect of supposing the corruption to have taken place in the words "as little," and read,

> I have a heart *to kindle* apt as yours,
> But yet a brain that leads my use of anger
> To better vantage.

The word *kindle* occurs twice before in the same tragedy:

> "This is the way to kindle, not to quench."

says Menenius to the tribunes.

The transition, however, from *to kindle* to the received reading *as little*, is not easy to imagine, and the suggested reading consequently is not entitled to more than to be held in doubt with the rest of the conjectures I have cited.

On a review of what has been said, it is plain that the crucial circumstance is here wanting. Amidst the abundance of actual and possible suggestions, we find no distinctive ground for determining with positiveness what the reading ought to be, although we may safely reject, I think, the feeble emendation of the Perkins folio.

TIMON OF ATHENS.

ALMOST innumerable other examples, to illustrate the subject in hand, might be selected from the annotations of editors as well as from the manuscript corrections of the old Perkins folio, which, as emendations, are plausible enough, but are deficient in any special claim to be received or to be preferred over others equally plausible. From the notice which the latter corrections have attracted, I am induced to animadvert upon a few more that come under this description.

The passage which first offers itself to my hand is from "Timon of Athens;" I quote it as usually given:

> "I have a tree, which grows here in my close,
> That mine own use invites me to cut down,
> And shortly must I fell it: tell my friends,
> Tell Athens, in the sequence of degree,
> From high to low throughout, that whoso please
> To stop affliction, *let him take his haste*,
> Come hither, ere my tree hath felt the axe,
> And hang himself." Act v. sc. 2.

The expression to *take haste** is certainly not to be found in any other place in the poet's writings, and I never met with it any where else. He constantly uses *make* haste. Singularly enough, it has not attracted the attention of any of the commentators in Boswell. For the half line in italics the old corrector proposes to substitute,

> To stop affliction *let him take his halter,*

which Mr. Collier says he is convinced is the genuine language of Shakespeare. See preface to "Seven Lectures on Shakespeare and Milton," page lxxx.

The proposed emendation is intrinsically good: it removes an awkward expression which could hardly have proceeded from the poet, but we might, I think, hit upon other emendations falling in more aptly with the course of thought, and quite as likely, or even more likely, to be perverted into the actual reading.

It is plain that the dominant point intimated in the sarcastic recommendation of the speaker, is that his countrymen should use *despatch* in availing themselves of his generous offer. He tells the senators that he must shortly fell the tree, and that consequently no time is to be lost in the matter.

* It is worthy of notice, that although we do not say *take haste,* yet when we wish to express the opposite idea we say *take time,—let him take his time.* It is possible that this idiom might have suggested the phrase in the text.

To name the instrument, whether sash, or halter, or scarf, or handkerchief, is unimportant to the purpose in view, while to urge haste just at this point is essential to the force of the irony.

This end is effected in the following modification of the line:

> To stop affliction, let him *make wise* haste,

which would have been more readily corruptible into *take his haste*, than the correction proposed in the old folio.

As a number of other epithets, however, might be severally prefixed to *haste*, all occasionally used by Shakespeare in connection with that noun, as well as with the verb *make*, and none of them having any decided claim to preference over its brother-monosyllables, such as *quick*, *hot*, *post*, *swift*, we can only class the reading as indeterminate. If the one I have selected (*wise*) has any superiority, it is in being perhaps more ironical, and coming nearer in sound to *his* than the rest.

After all, however, is it needful to do more than change *take* his haste into *make* his haste? In "Antony and Cleopatra," Antony says to Octavia, who is anxious to reconcile the two rivals,

> "But as you requested,
> Yourself shall go between us; the meantime, lady,
> I'll raise the preparation of a war
> Shall stain your brother: *make your* soonest *haste*."

which proves that the phrase *make haste* was sometimes used with an intermediate possessive pronoun.

There is a singular use of *haste* in the same tragedy, which may be worth remarking. Cleopatra says to one of her attendants in reference to the fatal asp,

> "Hie thee again;
> I have spoke already and it is provided;
> Go, *put it to the haste.*" Act v. sc. 2.

HENRY IV.

A VIGOROUS passage occurs in "Henry IV." Part II. act iv. sc. 1, which appears to me to have sustained several disfigurements, two of them not noticed by the commentators, exemplifying the same inadvertent repetition of words (presumably by the copyist or compositor) which has elsewhere been or will be more particularly enlarged upon. A third portion of the received text has, on other grounds, been the subject of much dispute whether it is genuine or spurious, and it may be admitted, at the outset, that all the amendments now to be discussed are of a character which can scarcely aspire to a higher title than doubtful.

Westmoreland, on behalf of the King, is remonstrating with the contumacious Archbishop of York:

> "Wherefore do you so ill translate yourself
> Out of the speech of peace, that bears such grace,
> Into the harsh and boisterous *tongue of war;*
> Turning your books to grieves, your ink to blood,
> Your pens to lances, and your *tongue* divine,
> To a loud trumpet and *a point of war?*"

The first thing to allege in proving this passage to be corrupt, is the tasteless and unskilful repetition of the sonorous word *tongue* in the fifth line. We can hardly suppose it to have proceeded from Shakespeare, if we consider merely the phonic effect; and that impression is strengthened by discerning that the repeated word is first used in the sense of *language*, and secondly in the sense of the *organ of speech*. I would suggest the substitution of *voice* for the second *tongue*, not only as obviating the defects indicated, but as better suiting the epithet *divine*. This suggestion receives support from the next scene, where Prince John, harping on the same string, styles the Archbishop,

> "To us the imagin'd *voice* of God himself."

And throughout the Bible (it may be added), *voice* is the term uniformly employed in reference to the Supreme Being.

It will be observed, on looking at the ends of the third and sixth lines, that there is a double occurrence also of the phrase *of war*, the first very much impairing, by pre-occupation of the ear, the sonorous force of the close — a defect which might be remedied by eliminating *war* from the third line, and inserting *strife* in its place. Any reader who attends to the cadence of the two lines must, I imagine, be sensible of a disagreeable monotony in their inflection, and the proposed substitution would not only obviate the sameness, but do it by a word often applied by Shakespeare to designate intestine broils.

Besides the separate bad effects of the two repetitions, both are so mixed together that the music of the lines is inartistically jangled in a style anything but Shakespearian; all which defects the suggested corrections in combination would rectify.

The last thing to note, in the passage before us, is the word *point* — *point of war* — which is here interpreted by Dr. Johnson to signify *tune*. Objections have been frequently made to it, but the phrase is well defended by Mr. Dyce, who affirms that it is not an uncommon expression, and quotes an example of its use from Greene's "Orlando Furioso:"

> "Tell him from me, false coward as he is,
> That Orlando, the County Palatine,
> Is come this morning with a band of French,
> To play him hunt's-up with a *point of war*," &c.

He also cites another instance, from Peele's "Edward I.," as follows:

> "Matrevers, thou
> Sound proudly here a perfect *point of war*
> In honour of thy sovereign's safe return."
> *Dyce's Ed.* 1861, p. 378.

These instances undoubtedly prove that the term was in use in that age, and seem, at first sight, amply sufficient to prevent the received reading from being disturbed. On the other side, it may be urged that the phrase does not occur elsewhere in Shakespeare's works, and therefore, like all remarkable phrases in the same predicament, can maintain its position only by its peculiar appropriateness. Amidst his frequent descriptions of battles and sieges and encampments, it seems scarcely probable that he should have used so notable an expression only once, and then with no special felicity.* The old corrector and Mr. Singer have each proposed a substitute for *point;* the first suggests *report*, the second *bruit:* but these suggestions have met with so little favour that it is needless to discuss them. Both writers have missed a much more plausible emendation, namely, the substitution of *portént* for *a point* as follows,

To a loud trumpet and portént of war.

Portent is frequently used by our author and always, as far as I can find, with the accent on the second syllable. In the first part of this play of

* I say with no special felicity, because to designate the Archbishop's voice a *point of war* as well as a *trumpet* would be to describe it in the same breath as both a musical instrument and the tune played upon it. Nevertheless, it is a pretty and even poetical phrase, and therefore we need not wonder that it was caught up by Sir Walter Scott in "Waverley," "The trumpets and kettledrums of the cavalry were next heard to perform the beautiful and wild *point of war* appropriated as a signal for that piece of nocturnal duty, and then finally sank upon the wind with a shrill and mournful cadence." I have taken this extract from the Supplement to Dr. Richardson's Dictionary.

"Henry IV." we have a passage corresponding in some respects to the remonstrance of the Earl of Westmoreland with the contumacious Archbishop, already quoted, and which makes greatly in favour of the suggested reading. It is a remonstrance of the King himself with the Earl of Worcester, one of the rebellious Percies and uncle to the redoubted Hotspur, in which he stigmatises the Earl (as my emendation would the Churchman) as a portent of coming evil.

> "Will you again unknit
> This churlish knot of all abhorrèd war,
> And move in that obedient orb again,
> When you did give a fair and natural light,
> And be no more an exhal'd meteor,
> A prodigy of fear, and *a portént*
> Of broachèd mischief to the unborn times?"

Let me now gather up my proposed emendations including this last one, and try how they look together:

> Wherefore do you so ill translate yourself
> Out of the speech of peace that bears such grace
> Into the harsh and boisterous tongue of *strife;*
> Turning your books to grieves, your ink to blood,
> Your pens to lances, and your *voice* divine,
> To a loud trumpet and *portént* of war.

My suggestion regarding the last line may perhaps be strengthened by the following address of King John, in the play of that name, to Chatillon the French Ambassador, who had just bidden him defiance in the name of his master:—

"Bear mine to him and so depart in peace:
Be thou as lightning in the eyes of France;
For ere thou can'st report I will be there,
The thunder of my cannon shall be heard:
So hence! Be thou the *trumpet* of my wrath,
And sullen *presage* of your own decay."

Another passage also gives us *trumpet* in connexion with the premonitory function of the instrument:

"The southern wind
Doth play the *trumpet* to his purposes,
And by his hollow whistling in the leaves
Foretells a tempest and a blustering day.
Henry IV. Part I. act v. sc. 1.

I can, however, adduce these extracts only to show that if *point of war* were set aside there might be a better substitute than either *bruit* or *report.* At present I regard the reading of the whole passage as doubtful.

The following is another apparently happy correction, which will not however stand the proposed tests, and since rival emendations of equal plausibility may be suggested it must be considered doubtful. In "Henry IV." Part II. there are some lines at the end of Scroop's speech, in which, as given in the received text, a manifest error appears, which could scarcely have come from the author's pen:—

"So that this land, like an offensive wife
That hath enraged *him on* to offer strokes,
As he is striking, holds his infant up,
And hangs resolved correction in the arm
That was uprear'd to execution." Act iv. sc. 1.

The simile here being of course intended to be complete in itself, the pronoun *him* is without antecedent, and the defect mars a very graphic picture. The old corrector alters the second line to : —

> "That hath enraged *her man* to offer strokes,"

which completely rectifies the error; nor does any great difficulty present itself, in conceiving how the substitution arose. On the other hand there are reasons for concluding that the erroneous reading is to be found in the first, not the second line *Offensive wife* is scarcely Shakespeare's diction; the epithet is used by him in only one other place, and there applied to *things* not persons. That solitary instance occurs in "Lear." Oswald, when addressing Goneril in reference to her husband, says,

> "What most he should dislike seems pleasant to him;
> What like, offensive."

Further the noun *man* substituted in the second line is not a Shakespearian synonyme for *husband*. In one passage, the compound *good·man* is found in the sense of husband, but *man* by itself, in that sense (unless I am greatly deceived), nowhere. Besides, *enraged to offer* is far less expressive than *enraged on to offer*, which implies accumulated provocation, and palliates in some degree (if any thing can palliate) the unmanliness of the imaginary wife-beater. Dropping the *on* damages the force and the poetry of the line.

The suggestion I have to make preserves the significant particle and rectifies the anomaly of a pronoun looking blank for want of an antecedent to keep it in countenance, quite as effectually as the old annotator's correction, which extinguishes the pronoun and the want together. I propose to read :

> So that this land, like a *man's peevish* wife
> That hath enraged him on to offer strokes,
> As he is striking, holds his infant up
> And hangs resolv'd corrèction in the arm
> That was uprear'd to execution.

In favour of this suggestion I would further point out that the comparison of the land [*England*] to *a man's peevish wife*, is far more appropriate than to an *offensive wife*, the latter not properly symbolising the relation of the kingdom to the king. When King John, in the play of that name, is with his troops before Angiers, which would submit to neither English nor French, Falconbridge styles it *this peevish town*.

The epithet in question is also employed by the poet in divers other places. The resemblance between the two locutions *a man's peevish* and *an offensive*, is, indeed, small enough. Possibly the compositor's eye caught the letters *offe* from the line below. Another weak side may be found too in the emendation. Several epithets equally plausible perhaps with *peevish*, might be prefixed to wife, such as *froward* or *envious*, and with any of these epithets the suggested alteration would be superior to the manuscript correction in the Perkins folio, but such a plurality of rival readings without marked superiority in any, necessarily renders the genuine one uncertain. Nor is it clear to everybody beyond dispute that the anomaly of a pronoun without an antecedent did not originate with Shakespeare himself. Mr. Dyce pronounces the correction in the Perkins folio, "as not only quite unnecessary, but as one of the corrector's very worst conjectures," an opinion, however, which he does not vindicate by a single reason.* Mr. Singer, on the other hand, says, "The substitution of *her man* for *him on* at the end of Scroop's speech, is a very plausible correction, and is evidently called for. This may be considered one of the corrector's few admissible conjectures."† Since neither of these critics assigns the grounds of his conclusion, neither of them helps us to come to a decision.

* "The Works of William Shakespeare," vol. iii. p. 552.

† "The Text of Shakespeare Vindicated," p. 117.

HENRY V.

The following description of Falstaff on his death-bed has given rise to much comment and controversy. The Hostess is the speaker: "after I saw him fumble with the sheets, and play with flowers, and smile upon his fingers' ends, I knew there was but one way; for his nose was sharp as a pen *and a table of green fields.*" "Henry V." act ii. sc. 3.

The expression in italics, which is not to be found in the quarto editions of 1600 and 1608, first appears in the folio of 1623, and is universally pronounced to be spurious. Theobald introduced the extraordinary correction, *and 'a babbled of green fields,*" which has been generally adopted.

The favoured emendation seems to me not only to have no support whatever in the context but to be quite discordant with it. It has doubtless been recommended by its prettiness and the supposed ease with which *'a babbled* might have been perverted into *a table.*

On the other hand *babbling of green fields* is

inconsistent with the rest of the talk ascribed to him; for immediately after the expression in dispute, the Hostess proceeds to tell her audience that he cried out God three or four times: he "bade me," she adds, "lay more clothes on his feet:" and we are further informed that "he cried out of sack:" he affirmed women were devils incarnate: he said once the devil would have him about women: he talked about the whore of Babylon: he saw a flea stick upon Bardolph's nose, and said it was a black soul burning in hell. These are the particular details of his last moments. Amidst such topics, such images, and such language, reported partly by the Hostess and partly by the Boy to have been the utterances of Falstaff *immediately before death*, what place is there for *babbling of green fields?*

Several suggestions with a view to correct the wrong reading, have been brought forward, for the particulars of which I must refer to the Variorum Edition. One commentator supposes it to have originated in a marginal direction having slided into the text, for which supposition there appear to be no grounds: another proposes to read *on a table of green fells*, meaning a table-book with a shagreen cover.

This — perhaps the likeliest of all the proposals — might be rendered still more likely by substituting *greasy* for *green*, and putting *fell* in the singular number; which alterations would transform the passage into "his nose was as sharp as a pen on a table [or tablet] of greasy fell."

Even the correction thus modified has so little probability in its favour that it is scarcely worth while referring to any other passages by way of support or invalidation. *Greasy fells* is a phrase in "As You Like It," but applied to living ewes with the fells still on their backs*, and it is not to be found elsewhere. In the use of the epithet there may be supposed to have been a covert reference to the personal condition of Falstaff himself, who in one place ("Merry Wives" act ii. sc. i.) is called a *greasy knight*, and in another ("Henry IV." Part I. act ii. sc. iv.) an *obscene greasy tallow-keech*. It may also be said that there is at least congruity in connecting *pen* and *tablet* of parchment †, and none in connecting *pen*, *table*, and *green fields*.

The emendation is, nevertheless, not satisfactory; and the same may be said of the one registered in the Perkins folio: "his nose was as sharp as a pen on a table of *green frieze*." Why should the sharpness of a pen be coupled with the covering of a wooden table? And the question here put leads me to remark that strict congruity seems to require the nose to be compared in point

* "Is not parchment made of sheep-skins?" asks Hamlet, act v. sc. 1.

† King John on *his* deathbed utters a curious expression "I am a scribbled form, drawn with a pen upon a parchment."

of sharpness to something which projects from a surface, as the gnomon of a dial.

It will be concluded from this discussion, that the reading of the passage must be set down as indeterminate; though "the babbling of green fields" should certainly not be kept up.

HENRY VI.

THE passage I have next to cite can scarcely be brought under the head of indeterminate, but since it has given rise to a correction in the Perkins folio, not only needless but easily driven from the field by competitors, and deservedly condemned by the generality of critics, I do not know that I can find a more appropriate place for it.

It furnishes us with a sample of the quality of those whole lines which are occasionally interpolated by the manuscript corrector.

The passage referred to forms part of Gloucester's reply to the King Henry the Sixth's requisition that he should give up his staff of office. The received reading is,

> "My staff? here, noble Henry, is my staff;
> As willingly do I the same resign,
> As e'er thy father, Henry, made it mine;
> And even as willingly at thy feet I leave it,
> As others would ambitiously receive it."
>
> *Henry VI.* Part II. act ii. sc. 3.

The corrector after the first line, introduces another to make up with it a rhyming couplet :

"To think I fain would keep it makes me laugh."

Here, it may at the outset be remarked, there is no proper starting-place for emendation, no call to tamper with the received text: there is no fault to correct in the sense, and there is certainly no necessity to supply the blank in the rhyme, for the sake of making the passage correspond with the rest of the dialogue, where rhyme and blank verse alternate without rule. But were the case otherwise there remains the fundamental objection to the interpolated line that it does not fall in with the tone of the context. Not only is it feeble but it jars on the feelings like a discord on the ear. Nor is this all. I find on proceeding to apply the other *criteria* to the correction that the mere words of the addition are Shakespearian enough, but there is no special reason why this particular line should be added rather than any one of half a dozen other lines which might be devised to complete the couplet equally well.

For instance, the supposed deficiency in the verse might be supplied as follows:

My staff? here, noble Henry, is my staff,
I never held it on my own behalf.

A line which if not perfect in point of rhyme, would at least have the merit of harmonising better with the spirit of the speaker; but which at the same time I am bound to admit there are no grounds whatever for believing Shakespeare to have written.

I may here take occasion to observe that whenever the old corrector of the Perkins folio ventures on the interpolation of a whole line (an experiment trying enough to any one's intellectual vigour when the task is to eke out the composition of Shakespeare) his attempts are, as far as I have examined them, and I think I have missed none, alike unsuccessful and almost uniformly feeble.

This is important, because as he adduces no extrinsic considerations to prove the interpolated lines to be the legitimate progeny of our great poet, the only possible circumstance to throw upon them a colour of genuineness is their intrinsic excellence. Whole lines invented to fill up vacancies left by lost ones must in the nature of the case be destitute of the same kind of evidence as offers itself for single phrases, and it is not easy to devise a combination of circumstances which would take any of them out of the category of mere conjectures.

HENRY VIII.

THE Perkins folio proposes a correction of the following passage in "Henry VIII." in which a phrase is manifestly corrupt. It represents Anne Boleyn speaking to a friend, an old lady, who had just been rallying her on her sudden elevation to the rank and title of the Marchioness of Pembroke:

> "Good lady,
> Make yourself mirth with your particular fancy,
> And leave me out on't. Would I had no being,
> If this *salute* my blood a jot; it faints me
> To think what follows." Act ii. sc. 3.

"Whatever meaning," says Mr. Collier, "may be attached to the expression *salute my blood*, the sense of the poet is rendered much more distinct if we substitute a different word easily misread or misprinted:—

> Would I had no being,
> If this *elate* my blood a jot.

"*Elate*," Mr. Collier continues, "as an adjective, is of very old use in our language, and it is doing no great violence to Shakespeare to suppose that here he converted an adjective into a verb."* He then states it to be one of the corrections made in the Perkins folio.

Even Mr. Singer thinks this emendation specious, although, as he remarks, "we have no other instance of Shakespeare's use of the word either as a verb or an adjective."

Thus on the one hand it may be urged that the word here proposed is not Shakespearian and also that it is unusual with writers generally to talk of elating the blood by exaltation of rank, or any other gratifying incident. We speak of warming and quickening the blood and of elating or elevating the spirits. For these reasons the emendation cannot be said to command the assent by its eminent felicity.

On the other hand, we say of an angry man his blood is up, and our author makes Hotspur address his followers in similar phraseology :—

"Fellows, soldiers, friends,
Better consider what you have to do,
Than I that have not well the gift of tongue,
Can *lift your blood up* with persuasion."
Henry IV. Part I. act v. sc. 2.

Another reading has suggested itself to me, the transition from which to the received text would be easy :

If this *shall heat* my blood a jot.

---

* "Notes and Emendations," 2nd edition p. 325.

Against which there is certainly the objection that the verb here is better in the present tense, while the whole plausibility of my suggestion depends on its being in the future, the emendation assuming that *shall heat* has lapsed into *salute.* Amidst these hostile considerations the reading I think may be held as dubious.

MUCH ADO ABOUT NOTHING.

In "Much Ado about Nothing" there is a word used by Dogberry which has given rise to some discussion.

The sapient constable, having been called an ass, recalcitrates in a well-known passage, and, amongst other boasts, says—

> "I am a wise fellow; and which is more, an officer; and which is more, a householder; and which is more, as pretty a piece of flesh as any in Messina; and one that knows the law, go to; and a rich fellow enough, go to; and a fellow that hath *had losses;* and one that hath two gowns, and everything handsome about him." Act iv. sc. 2.

The expression *had losses* seems away from the purpose, as the man is enumerating his claims to consideration, and losses can scarcely be regarded in that light. To substitute *leases*, as proposed by the Perkins folio, would be adopting an alteration quite destitute of appropriateness. I have two rival suggestions to offer: (1) that the true reading is *horses*, or *hosses*—a perversion of *horses* now, at least, widely prevailing both in town and country amongst persons of Dogberry's rank. It seems quite in character that the "officer" and "householder," in repudiating the appellation of *ass*, should allege, as a point blank contradiction, that he himself had kept *horses*. How could an ass have been the master of those superior animals? The logic is irresistible. I suspect, however, that this particular boast, like the rest, ought to be in the present tense, and that *had* was inserted to make sense of *losses*. It is more congruous to say, "and a fellow that *hath horses*."

But horses after all are rather too magnificent a possession for Dogberry, and it would be a sad anti-climax to descend from such a vaunt to the boast of two gowns. In order to prepare *secundum artem* for the latter, we ought to find a still humbler garment. I venture therefore, if my first suggestion be rejected—in which I am disposed to concur—(2) to propose *trossers* in its place:

a rich fellow enough, go to; and a fellow that hath *trossers;* and one that hath two gowns, and everything handsome about him.

Trossers or *trowses* is a word, we are told, that is very frequently met with in our old dramatic writers, and it occurs once in Shakespeare, coupled with the epithet *strait*, to denote tight breeches.

Had losses may possibly have been converted from *strait trossers.**

Taking into view all the emendations suggested, we can go no farther, I think, than discard *had losses*, and leave the other proposals undecided.

* In Nares's "Glossary" a quotation is given, under this word, which says of the Irish: "Their *trowses* commonly spelt *trossers*, were long pantaloons, exactly fitted to the shape." Malone's Shakespeare, Boswell's Edition, vol. xvii. p. 376, contains a long train of notes and references on the same topic.

A MIDSUMMER-NIGHT'S DREAM.

The next example that I shall select is from "A Midsummer-Night's Dream."

Theseus is commenting on the "brief" or catalogue of sports to be played before him and the rest of the company. He comes to—

> "A tedious brief scene of young Pyramus
> And his love, Thisbe; very tragical mirth."

On which he exclaims—

> "Merry and tragical! tedious and brief!
> That is—hot ice, and wondrous *strange* snow."

All sorts of epithets have been proposed to replace *strange*, which falls flat on the ear, and manifestly does not form the requisite antithesis with snow. *Scorching*, *strong*, *black*, *seething*, *strange black*, *swarthy*, have all found advocates. The desideratum seems, at first sight, plain enough. As ice is the type of cold, so snow is usually the type of whiteness, and the natural antithesis or rather contradictory combination being in the first case *hot ice*, ought in the second to be *black snow*. But then there is no discernible way in which *black* could have been perverted into *strange*,—an objection partially, indeed, removed by substituting *raven*, which Shakespeare uses elsewhere in contrast with snow. In "Romeo and Juliet" occurs the expression, "whiter than new snow on a raven's back." The line in question would then be—

That is—hot ice and wondrous *raven* snow.

There is, however, a strong argument against the supposition that this, the most natural and simple antithesis, was the one intended; and that is the application of the epithet *wondrous;* for if the reading were *black* or *raven snow* there would be nothing certainly more wonderful in that than in *hot ice*, and the epithet in question ought to have ushered in the latter. To prefix it to the second contradictory combination, and not to the first, would show want of skill or tact in the poet.

As Shakespeare seldom used or placed an epithet without a good reason for it, there is a probability that *wondrous* was intended as a sarcastic allusion to some marvellous traveller's story recently given to the world, and describing a country covered with some highly tinted snow, such as crimson, or golden, or cerulean. Cardan, who died when Shakespeare was a boy, stated in one of his books that *blue* snow was common near the Straits of

Magellan; and to come to more recent times, thirty or forty years ago Captains Ross and Parry reported that they had met with red or *pink* snow* —a phenomenon subsequently confirmed by others. It is not, therefore, an outrageous supposition that some voyager in Shakespeare's days had brought back an account of having seen snow of a red or golden colour, and that the passage before us is a sly fling at the marvellous, and at that time perhaps incredible, tale. If we adopt this theory the reading is easily set right:

"hot ice and wondrous *strange* snow,"

becomes

hot ice and wondrous *orange* snow.

The only change here is the substitution of *o* for *st*, with the advantage to the metre of *wondrous* being reinstated in its character of a dissyllable, whereas in the received text it must be read as a trisyllable, *won-der-ous*.†

* These facts are mentioned in Mr. Hunter's "New Illustrations of Shakespeare," vol. i. p. 142, where he cites them in quite a different connection. I have never had an opportunity of looking into Cardan.

† "The extraordinary phenomenon of *red snow* observed by Captain Ross and other Arctic voyagers naturally excited the greatest interest both at home and abroad. This singular aspect of a substance with which we never fail to associate an idea of the purest and most radiant whiteness, has been ascertained to result from an assemblage of very minute vegetable bodies, belonging to the class of cryptogamic plants, and the

I must fairly own, however, that this reading can scarcely be considered as more than possibly right unless some antecedent or contemporary traveller's account can be produced of such a marvellous phenomenon.

What also makes against it is, that *orange-tawney* was then the adjective employed to designate the colour in question, not simply *orange*.

As moreover there was, as already stated, a tale extant at that time about *blue* snow, the line in the above extract might have reference to that alleged phenomenon, and the epithet employed to describe it might have been *azure*. We thus have three readings besides those of the commentators:

That is—hot ice and wondrous orange snow.
" " " raven snow.*.
" " " azure snow.

---

natural order called *Algæ*. They form the species named *Protococcus nivalis* by Agardh, which is synonymous with the *Uredo nivalis* of Mr. Bauer." . . . . "There is no reason to suppose that the colouring matter itself, as well as the snow, is a meteorological product, although Humboldt certainly mentions a shower of red hail which fell at Paramo de Guanacos in South America." "Mr. Scoresby conjectured that the red colour of the Arctic snow derived its origin from innumerable multitudes of very minute creatures belonging to the order *Radiata*. He had frequently observed the ice to be tinged with *an orange colour*, obviously resulting from an assemblage of small transparent animals."—*Discovery and Adventure in the Polar Seas and Regions*, pp. 107, 108, 110.

* Another reading has occurred to me, since the text was written, instead of *raven*, equally denoting black, and perhaps equally convertible into *strange*,—namely, *sable*.

The word *orange* would be the most easily perverted into *strange;* but the transformation of *raven* or *azure* into that epithet would not be difficult.

On a retrospect of the various suggestions which have been thrown out in regard to this one designation, we may well pronounce the reading indeterminate.

ALL'S WELL THAT ENDS WELL.

The passage which I have next to bring forward may possibly show how an expression in one place sometimes serves to correct a wrong reading in another.

In "All's Well that Ends Well," act iii. sc. 2, Helena, apostrophising Rousillon, says:—

> "Poor lord! is 't I
> That chase thee from thy country, and expose
> Those tender limbs of thine to the event
> Of the none-sparing war? and is it I
> That drive thee from the sportive court, where thou
> Wast shot at with fair eyes, to be the mark
> Of smoky muskets? O, you leaden messengers,
> That ride upon the violent speed of fire,
> Fly with false aim; *move* the *still-piecing* air
> That sings with *piercing*, do not touch my lord!"

Shakespeare would scarcely have used *piecing* (or *peering*, as the old folio, 1623, has it) and *piercing* in such close proximity. One of these words probably led to the erroneous insertion of the other. I suggest *still-closing* for *still-piecing*, and support it by the following lines from "The Tempest," act iii. sc. 3.

> "the elements,
> Of whom your swords are temper'd, may as well
> Wound the loud winds, or with bemock'd-at stabs
> Kill the *still-closing* waters."

Yet there is scarcely sufficient evidence in favour of the emendation to establish it and take it out of the present category, especially when we advert to the consideration that the passage, insignificant as it may seem, has been commented upon by Warburton, Steevens, Malone, Tyrwhitt, and Douce, most of whom are for the retention of still-piecing*, first introduced by an unnamed critic.

With regard to the preceding verb *move*, which it will be observed, is also in italics, the Perkins folio has proposed to substitute *wound*—a decided improvement on the received text, and not very remote in resemblance.† *Move* is certainly flat, and without particular significance where it is placed. Another reading has occurred to me—*cleave*—but although better than *move*, it is inferior to *wound* in appropriate meaning, and is not a term used by Shakespeare in reference to air or water, while *wound* has in its support the passage already cited from "The Tempest."

* See Malone's Shakespeare, by Boswell, vol. x. p. 406.

† Compare *wounde* (often so spelt) and the old form *moue.*

TWELFTH NIGHT.

In "Twelfth Night" we have another instance of indeterminate reading in the following passage: Sebastian is describing his sister Viola: —

"A lady, sir, though it was said she much resembled me, was yet of many accounted beautiful; but though I could not with *such estimable wonder over-far* believe that, yet thus far I will boldly publish her, — she bore a mind that envy could not but call fair." *

The words in italics are obviously destitute of meaning: they are mere nonsense, and could not have been written by Shakespeare. The Perkins folio presents us with the following emendation: —

"But though I could not with *self-estimation wander so far to* believe that, yet thus far I will boldly publish her."

Here the alteration is successful in restoring sense to the clause, maintains the tone of the composition, is consonant on the whole with Shake-

* "Twelfth Night," act ii. sc. 1.

speare's usual style of expression, and is so near in sound to the corrupt reading as to render the substitution of the latter sufficiently probable. Nevertheless it is not quite satisfactory; for not only is *self-estimation* a word not found in any other place, but other equally plausible emendations may be suggested. Mr. Singer brings forward a rival reading by another "old corrector," which strikes me as an improvement:—

"A lady, sir, though it was said she much resembled me, yet was of many accounted beautiful; but though I could not with *such estimators wander* over far *to* believe that, yet thus far will I boldly publish her," &c.

It unfortunately happens, nevertheless, for this emendation that the word *estimators* is not Shakespearian; and as it also does not come in with any particular felicity it may, on that ground, be set aside. But if we change *estimators* into *estimate* we shall adopt a term used familiarly by our author*, and at the same time make passable sense of Mr. Singer's reading:

I could not with *such estimate* wander over-far to believe that.

There is no particular harshness in saying that an "estimate wanders," *alias* "opinion errs," or that any one errs with it.

I should not have dwelt so long on this correc-

* "Of name and noble *estimate*."
Richard II. act ii. sc. 3.

tion of the Perkins folio, had it not been adduced by an able critic in the "Edinburgh Review" as a happy one. The conclusion to be drawn on a review of the whole argument is, I think, that the reading must come under the class which I am engaged in elucidating.

The comedy of "Twelfth Night" in a subsequent part contains another misreading, which has exercised the ingenuity of a number of annotators without any decisive result. It occurs in Act ii. sc. 5. I cannot perhaps introduce it more succinctly than in the words of Mr. Collier :—

"Fabian is enforcing silence in order that Malvolio, while they are watching him, may not discover them, and says in the folio 1623—'Though our silence be drawn from us with *cars*, yet peace!' The folio 1632 prints 'cars' *cares*, and many proposals have been made to alter 'cars' to *cables*, *carts*, &c.; but 'with cars' turns out to be an error of the press for *by th' ears*, or *by the ears*, and the meaning is perfectly clear when we read, 'Though our silence be drawn from us *by th' ears*, yet peace!'"

Mr. Singer, who justly terms this a most improbable phrase, is not happy in his own suggestion—"with tears." The proposed emendation, however, of the Perkins folio is more than improbable,—it is utterly devoid of appropriate meaning.*

* There is a part of the dialogue between the Prince and Falstaff in "King Henry IV." Part II. act ii. sc. 4, which

The poet is talking figuratively of *silence* being drawn from the persons in the scene, instead of *sounds* being drawn from them. He is in fact employing the same terms in regard to silence as we usually employ with regard to a secret; and when did anyone speak of drawing a secret, or indeed utterances of any kind, from another "by the ears." We usually look to the tongue as the organ through which such communications are to come.

Nothing can be plainer than the speaker's intention to enjoin in a strain of half-humorous exaggeration, that his comrades should preserve silence, even though the utmost violence should be employed to make them break it, though, in fact, they should be put to the torture. This was meant to be expressed in the curt way alone practicable under the circumstances by some monosyllable which *cars* has unfortunately displaced, and which it is our business to recover. If we read *screws* instead of *cars* the restoration will, if I mistake not, be accomplished. "Though our silence should be drawn from us with *screws*, yet peace!"

may seem at first sight to countenance this reading. Falstaff says to the Prince—"I am a gentleman, thou art a drawer;" to which the latter replies, "Very true, sir; and I come to draw you out by the cars." But to make this bear upon the case, silence must be supposed to be drawn out of Fabian and his companions by her own cars—a somewhat violent metaphor.

So late as the days of Shakespeare, and even later, judicial torture for the purpose of extorting confessions was not obsolete, and we find sundry allusions to it in his dramas. Long after the preceding emendation had struck me, I was pleased to find that the late Mr. Sidney Walker had proposed to read *racks**, which as completely suits in point of meaning as my own suggestion, but is liable to certain objections. *Racks* would not perhaps have been so easily perverted into *cars* as *screws* would; and on looking at the context we shall see that, if the proposed noun were inserted, the singular number with the definite article would be required to square with common usage: we should have to read *the rack*, not *racks*, in consequence of which the proposed emendation would be farther removed from probability.

On the other hand the term *rack* occurs a number of times in the plays (once or twice in the plural), and is evidently a familiar phrase, while the noun *screw* does not occur once, and the paronymous verb only twice, in neither case with any reference to torture. An instance of the use of the former word presents itself in the "Merchant of Venice," act iii. sc. 2.

> "*Portia.* Ay, but, I fear, you speak upon the rack,
> Where men enforcèd do speak any thing."

Giving all these considerations their due weight,

* "A Critical Examination of the Text of Shakespeare."

although I still retain a father's preference for *screws*, I think the reading cannot be regarded as otherwise than undetermined.

It is fair to add, that there is one passage in another play which has been cited as favourable to the received reading: Launce in the "Two Gentlemen of Verona" (act iii. sc. 1) says—

> "I am in love, but a team of horse shall not pluck that from me."

Surely, however, drawing with a team of horse—an every day operation—is not drawing with *cars*, which no one ever witnessed. Those vehicles, although they may be convenient machines for carriage, are clearly not instruments of draught.

THE WINTER'S TALE.

AMONGST the minor alleged corruptions in the text, there is one, consisting of a single monosyllable, about which Sir J. Hanmer, Dr. Warburton, Dr. Thirlby, Dr. Johnson, Mr. Steevens, Mr. Malone, Mr. John Mitford, Mr. Singer, Mr. Dyce, and the old corrector of the Perkins folio, or rather his editor, with other critics, have all given us their several opinions. It occurs in "The Winter's Tale" (act. iv. sc. 3). Perdita says to Florizel:

> "Sir, my gracious lord,
> To chide at your extremes it not becomes me;
> O, pardon that I name them; your high self,
> The gracious mark o' the land, you have obscur'd
> With a swain's wearing; and me, poor lowly maid,
> Most goddess-like prank'd up: but that our feasts
> In every mess have folly, and the feeders
> Digest it with a custom, I should blush
> To see you so attired; *sworn*, I think,
> To show myself a glass."

Of the contending parties, some are for retaining *sworn;* others advocate *swoon;* others, *scorn;* and the corrector in the Perkins folio, seconded by

Mr. Collier, offers us *so worn*. It appears to me quite unlikely that Shakespeare wrote either *sworn* or *so worn*, neither of them having any particular appropriateness, or even tolerably clear sense. *Swoon* imports a rather too violent effect to be produced on a maiden by seeing in a mirror a dress of which every article was already known to her,—an objection not applicable to *scorn*, which is perhaps the "best of the bunch," although somewhat pointless, if not misfitting the context.

Since none of these suggestions can be considered perfectly satisfactory, I will hazard a still different one, namely, *frown*, which seems indeed less easily convertible into *sworn* than the rest, but contains all the same letters except the initial consonant, and every critic knows that *s* and *f* are frequently interchanged. All that I can further say in its favour is, that the fair speaker, having talked of *blushes*, might very naturally mention another phenomenon of her own face, and put *frowns* in antithesis with them:

> I should *blush*
> To see you so attired; *frown*, I think,
> To show myself a glass.

But there is another way of dealing with the passage. The phrase *I think*, looks very much like an excrescence in any of these readings: why use it after *frown* rather than after *blush?* The natural course of thought would be, "I should blush to see you so attired, and recoil from looking at myself in a mirror." To get quit, then, of this superfluous phrase and express the natural sequence of ideas, we might read:

> I should blush
> To see you so attired; sorely shrink
> To show myself i' th' glass.

This emendation, however, is by no means so felicitous as to command adoption, or to preclude me from a further attempt.

When no decisively happy reading has been hit upon, emendations are apt to multiply themselves in conception without end. Another has just occurred to me, which has the recommendation of retaining and imbuing with significance the phrase *I think*, and is, perhaps, superior in simplicity to any hitherto mentioned:

> I should blush
> To see you so attired *; *more,* I think,
> To show myself a glass;

or perhaps better *i' th' glass.* Here the train of thought seems perfectly natural: "I should blush to see you dressed like a swain, and blush still more I think, to view myself in the glass prank'd-up like a goddess." The phrase *I think*, becomes less out of place, or rather surrenders its character

* One of the commentators—Mr. Walker, if I recollect right—has made the just remark that it is not necessary to read attirèd, as the word was probably intended to be pronounced att-i-erd.

of a patch, and the required incident of the word *more* lapsing into *sworn* (probably through the intermediate form *swore*), is easily conceivable.

Nevertheless, the passage, after all is said, cannot be rescued from the rank of doubtful without more light or more sagacity than any one has hitherto shown himself to possess. I prefer the last proposed emendation, on the whole, as the simplest and most appropriate to the speaker.

PART IV.

VERBAL REPETITIONS.

SINCE there appears to be some difference of opinion, how far the repetition of a word is to be considered an indication of spuriousness in the received text of Shakespeare's Plays, I purpose to discuss the question in the present chapter.

It must be admitted at the outset, that when a word which has been once used is, without apparent reason, used again before the sound of the first has had time to fade from the ear, the effect is generally felt to be displeasing. Every one has probably noticed the disagreeable impression so produced on himself and others. I have personally remarked such sensitiveness in actual life hundreds of times. It has, for example, frequently happened to myself, while I have been dictating to a secretary in the presence of friends interested in what was going on, and have inadvertently made use of the same expression twice in one sentence, that some one or other of the auditors, not perhaps remarkable for literary fastidiousness, has called my attention to the repetition by observing, "you have had that word before."

I mention this trivial circumstance to show the prevalence of distaste for such verbal repetition as occurs without apparent reason, even amongst those who do not cultivate style; and I scarcely need to add that, amongst those who do, it is regarded as a blemish in composition, and habitually shunned by the practised writer.*

We must, then, consider it in this light when it is found in Shakespeare; and since we cannot suppose him inferior to ordinary men in nicety of taste or in sensibility to (if I may so apply a scientific term) the interference of sounds, we may safely conclude that he would instinctively, if not systematically, avoid it. Hence the passages of his writings in which it appears without special reason, and in a way to offend the ear, may be set down as so far spurious. A few examples may be cited where this conclusion seems inevitable.

The following occurs in "As You Like It"

* One eminent writer within my recollection systematically adopted the practice of repeating a word or a phrase, whenever the least ambiguity was possible through employing a pronoun or other substitute. This, no doubt, rendered his composition clear and precise, but detracted from both its agreeableness and its force. I allude to Mr. John Austin, in his "Province of Jurisprudence Determined," first edition. A second edition, which I have not seen, has recently appeared.

(act v. sc. 2), in answer to the inquiry "what 'tis to love:"

> "It is to be all made of fantasy,
> All made of passion, and all made of wishes;
> All adoration, duty, and *observance;*
> All humbleness, all patience and impatience;
> All purity, all trial, all *observance.*"

From this clumsy iteration, every voice and pen unite to exonerate Shakespeare. It can be the result of nothing but miscopying or misprinting.

A no less palpable instance of the same fault presents itself in Part II. "Henry IV." (act i. sc. 1), where Travers is giving an account of what he saw and heard to the Earl of Northumberland. He had met with a horseman riding hard, who paused to tell him of Hotspur's death in battle:

> "With that he gave his *able* horse the head,
> And bending forward, struck his *able* heels
> Against the panting sides of his poor jade
> Up to the rowel head"—

another undisputed blunder either of the copyist or of the compositor, which no one thinks of imputing to the author of the play.

A third example may be cited from "Hamlet" (act ii. sc. 2). Polonius says to the King, according to the received text:

> "Give first admittance to the ambassadors;
> My *news* shall be the *news* to that great feast."

So evidently corrupt, that not a single editor, I believe, is found to defend it.

That the repetition in the preceding cases is not considered genuine, does not depend merely on the monotony or cacophony produced. In each case there is another defect. The occurrence of the word *observance* twice in the first-cited instance is sheer tautology, in itself displeasing; and the same may be said in regard to *news* in the third. In the second example, the application of the epithet *able* to *heels* is not tautological, but altogether inappropriate, and contrary to usage.

There are many cases, however, where the fault may be said to be pure. The double occurrence of a verb in the third and fourth lines of the following quotation (which I do not find noticed by any prior critic) is exceptionable, purely on the ground of its being a repetition, without that objection being, as in the preceding cases, mixed up with considerations of either tautology or inappropriateness. The same verb, it will be observed, occurs again both in the eighth and the tenth lines with unimpeachable propriety; so that the passage presents us with a specimen of genuine as well as of spurious recurrence of a word, in apposite illustration of the subject in hand:

"My name is Thomas Mowbray, Duke of Norfolk;
Who hither come engagèd by my oath
(Which God *defend* a knight should violate),
Both to *defend* my loyalty and truth
To God, my king, and his succeeding issue,
Against the Duke of Hereford that appeals me;

And, by the grace of God and this my arm,
To prove him, in *defending* of myself,
A traitor to my God, my king, and me:
And as I truly fight, *defend* me heaven!"
Richard II. act i. sc. 3.

Here, I think, the first *defend* has crept into the text from the eye of the compositor undesignedly catching the word from the line below. The term, it will be observed, is used in the two lines in two widely different senses, in both of which it was regularly employed in those days, and often by Shakespeare himself. The improbability is that he should employ the verb, with those two diverse significations (of which he must doubtless have been aware), in two successive lines, when there was a phrase at hand with the first signification, which he was more in the habit of using.

For the reasons assigned, I would suggest the reading,

My name is Thomas Mowbray, Duke of Norfolk;
Who hither come engagèd by my oath
(Which God *forbid* a knight should violate),
Both to *defend* my loyalty and truth.

The word *forfend* would answer the purpose equally well with *forbid*, and may at first sight seem preferable on account of its near resemblance to *defend;* but if I am right in my hypothesis as to the origin of the repetition, that circumstance is really not material; and, if it were, would be outweighed by the fact that Shakespeare uses the phrase *God forfend* only once, while his most usual phrase to express the same meaning is *God forbid.* It is remarkable, indeed, that in all other cases than that one, when he uses *forfend* in an invocation to supernal power, he joins it with *heaven* — *heaven forfend;* or with the plural of the divine name — *the Gods forfend.*

Spurious duplications, equally striking and equally incontrovertible, might be cited to an extent not generally suspected.* They have obviously arisen, or might have arisen, in the ordinary course of transcribing or putting into type.. Every one who has been concerned with copying or printing must have encountered or committed similar mistakes; and, considering the condition of authorship and of the press when Shakespeare's works were produced and published, it may be safely pronounced that the occurrence of numerous blunders of this class was inevitable. No kind of error is, in truth, more easy to commit.

There are repetitions, however, of a very different character from those which are justly held as indications of corruption; repetitions which claim to be genuine, and can show good cause why they make their appearance.

As the first-mentioned sort were unavoidable

* Mr. Walker adduces between one and two hundred instances, but a number of them I conceive may be shown to be genuine, and others of doubtful spuriousness. See his "Critical Examination," vol. i. p. 276.

from the channels and processes through which the plays made their way to the public, so those others were sure to occur in the regular course of authorship. In such an extensive range of composition as Shakespeare's works embrace, numerous occasions must arise in which the repetition of a word, so far from being a mistake on the part of copyist and compositor, would be introduced by the author himself because it was conducive to clearness, or emphasis, or compactness of expression, or to the complete bringing-out of a comparison, or antithesis, or point of wit, or turn of thought. Of this kind of duplication, which is, of course, always to be taken as genuine, and can seldom give rise to controversy, I will also adduce a few examples.

One of the simplest cases is the following, from the second part of "King Henry IV.," where the Prince is kneeling at the death-bed of his father, and explaining the rather premature act of taking away the crown. It contains two repetitions, both unexceptionable.

"If I do feign,
O, let me in my present wildness die,
And never live to show the incredulous world
The noble change that I have purposèd!
Coming to look on you, thinking you *dead*
(And *dead* almost, my liege, to think you were).
I spake unto the crown as having sense,
And thus upbraided it: 'The care on thee depending
Hath fed upon the body of my father;
Therefore thou best of *gold*, art worst of *gold*.'"

Act iv. sc. 4.

Here the natural play of thought could be effected only by the double employment of the respective terms.

I take next another repetition, the propriety of which is too evident to be enlarged upon. Hotspur ("Henry IV." Part I. act iv. sc. 1) is endeavouring to show the advantages of his father's absence on the approaching contest:

> "You strain too far.
> I rather of his absence make this use:—
> It lends a lustre and more great opinion,
> A larger dare to our great enterprise,
> Than if the earl were here; for men must think,
> If we, without his *help*, can make a head
> To push against the kingdom, with his *help*
> We shall o'erturn it topsy-turvy down."

To have varied the expression by substituting a synonyme (as *aid*, e.g.) would have weakened the antithesis as well as loosened that compactness or colligation of the sense which a recurrence of the same word frequently effects.

The following instance strikes me as well showing how iteration may contribute to the point of a sentiment. It is from "King John" (act iii. sc. 4). The dauphin Louis, in despair after the defeat of the French forces by the English, breaks out:

> "There's nothing in this world can make me joy:
> Life is as tedious as a twice-told tale
> Vexing the dull ear of a drowsy man;
> And *bitter shame* hath spoil'd the sweet world's taste,
> That it yields nought but *shame* and *bitterness*."

In regard to this repetition, I differ from Mr. Sidney Walker when he remarks, "Something is wanting that shall class with *bitterness; possibly gall.*" To myself, on the contrary, it appears that nothing is wanting. It is a complete expression of what was intended—a turn of sentiment rather than a play upon words, for which the repetition of both *shame* and *bitterness* is necessary. Not to insist on the pleonasm of coupling *gall*, as suggested, with the latter term, to take *shame* from the last verse and leave *bitterness*, as Mr. Walker is disposed to recommend, would spoil the point of the lines, whatever that may be worth, and only *half* extinguish the repetition. The latter (were it requisite) might be effectually and appropriately got rid of by saying,

> That it yields nought but gall and infamy;

but we have no grounds for such an alteration, while the actual reading is altogether in the poet's style, and well expresses a familiar truth,—that when we have suffered any bitter shame, the whole world is for us full of nothing else.

Whatever we may, in point of taste, think of the lines I shall next quote, it will be evident to all that every repetition in them is genuine. They form part of the lamentation of the Lady Anne over the corpse of Henry VI., in the tragedy of "Richard III.:"

> "O, *cursèd* be the hand that made these holes!
> *Cursèd* the *heart* that had the *heart* to do it!

> *Cursèd* the *blood* that let this *blood* from hence!
> More direful hap betide that hated *wretch*,
> That makes us *wretched* by the death of thee,
> Than I can wish to adders, spiders, toads,
> Or any creeping venom'd thing that lives!"

It would be difficult to find more decided examples than the foregoing lines present of repetition conspicuously genuine, both from the necessity of the sentiment and from an intentional play upon words.

I will cite one more instance in which there is good reason to suppose the verbal iteration to be genuine, premising that the first word put in italics is so distinguished for a different purpose, to be hereafter explained.

The Earl of Northumberland having just received the news of Hotspur's defeat and death, says to the messengers:

> "For this I shall have time enough to mourn.
> In poison there is physic; and these news,
> Having been well, that would have made me sick,
> Being sick, have in some measure made me well;
> And as the wretch, whose fever-weaken'd joints,
> Like strengthless hinges, *buckle* under life,
> Impatient of his fit, breaks like a fire
> Out of his keeper's arms; even so my limbs,
> Weaken'd with *grief*; being now enrag'd with *grief*,
> Are thrice themselves."

The substitution of *pain* for the first *grief* has been proposed. Not only, however, does there seem too little call for alteration to warrant a disturbance of the text (especially as abundance of authorities have been adduced for the use of the latter term in the sense of bodily suffering*), but the antithesis requires the repetition of the word:—*weakened* with grief is contrasted with *enraged* with grief, the contrast lying, not in the affection, but in the effects of it.

Having cited this speech, I take occasion to suggest the exchange of *buckle,* in the sixth line, for *knuckle.* Since the earl is talking of his limbs and joints, not of his armour (which comes afterwards), the latter of the terms in question seems to me the more appropriate of the two.

This is the only instance in which *buckle under,* in the sense of *bend under,* is attributed to Shakespeare, and I can find the phrase nowhere else; while, apart from any force of custom, which it appears not to have, it is in itself unmeaning — or, more properly, the combination of those two words is at variance with the usual signification of the first of them.

It may be alleged, indeed, that *knuckle under* has no precedent in Shakespeare, any more than *buckle under,*—which is true enough; but it has in its favour that it bears a strong affinity to joints, and that unlike *buckle under,* which is never met with, it may be heard amongst our peasantry and artizans even in the present day.

* Boswell's "Malone," vol. xvii. p. 17.

To return from this digression.

The preceding exposition has, if I mistake not, sufficed to show (1) that there are repetitions in Shakespeare which are decidedly spurious; and (2) that there are others which are as decidedly genuine; but, in addition to such, there are many which are so far dubious as to have formed subjects of controversy.

It may be instructive to notice a few of these.

The first I will cite occurs in "All's Well that Ends Well" (act i. sc. 3). The Countess of Rousillon is addressing Helen, who conceives she has the means of restoring the sick king to health:

"*Countess.*— But think you, Helen,
If you should tender your supposèd aid,
He would recéive it? He and his physicians
Are of a mind; he, that they cannot *help* him,
They, that they cannot *help*; how shall they credit
A poor unlearnèd virgin, when the schools,
Embowell'd of their doctrine, have left off
The danger to itself?"

"Evidently wrong," says Mr. Walker, "though I am not sure that cannot *heal* him is the true correction."

Most of the commentators pass this repetition without notice, but it can scarcely be genuine. If any reader will take the trouble of turning back to the instance already adduced of a legitimate repetition of the same word,* he will see that there is not the same reason for the iteration here. In the former case there was an antithesis to bring out, best done by identity of phrase; in the latter there is a unanimity to be set forth, which cannot be expressed without monotony except by varying the language.

I concur with Mr. Walker in not accepting the correction *cannot heal*, especially as a passage in the next act, sc. 3, assists us, I conceive, to the genuine reading. Helen, it may be premised, having, before this scene ensues, accomplished the cure of the king, a dialogue in reference to it takes place between Lafeu and Parolles. Lafeu has just said that the king had been "relinquished of all the learned and authentic fellows" (namely, the physicians), when the conversation proceeds:

* It is somewhat remarkable that I have had to call attention to three passages in which the word *help* is repeated. In two of them, one of the *helps* I have shown to be spurious, in the other, both to be genuine. There is a fourth passage noticed by Mr. Walker, which does not, perhaps, fairly come under the head of faulty recurrence, because the *helps* are separated by two lines of interrupted dialogue; but the first of them, as he has pointed out, is the wrong word. See "King Henry VI." Part II. act ii. sc. 1.

"Come offer at my shrine, and I will *help* thee."

There can scarcely be a doubt that the reading ought to be *heal thee*.

"*Parolles.* Right; so I say.
Lafeu. That gave him out *incurable*,——
Parolles. Why there it is; so say I too.
Lafeu. *Not to be helped*,——
Parolles. Right; as 't were a man assured of an ——
Lafeu. Uncertain life, and sure death."

Incurable and *not to be helped* seem to point to the genuine wording of the previous lines, also relating to the king's illness, and I accordingly propose to read:

He and his physicians
Are of a mind; he, that they cannot *help* him,
They, that they cannot *cure*.

For reasons not perhaps worth detailing, the substitution of the verb *cure* for *help* seems to come better in the last line than in the preceding one.

Another passage in the same play, condemned by Mr. Walker, may, I think, be retained as it is:

Bertram says to Helena (act ii. sc. 2):

"Prepared I was not
For such a business; therefore am I found
So much unsettled: this drives me to *entreat you*,
That presently you take your way for home,
And rather muse than ask why I *entreat you*."

I think it may be allowed to remain unaltered, on the ground that the monotony of the repetition is completely relieved by laying a proper emphasis on *why*, in the last line; so that the first *entreat you*, having in natural course the rising inflexion, the second *entreat you* may have the falling one.

Mr. Walker suggests *dismiss*, to replace the second; but the proper regulation of the emphasis (which, in fact, can scarcely be avoided) removes all objection on the score of taste, and appears to me to render the received reading more expressive than the lines would become by the substitution of another verb.

Besides, if we would get quit of the repetition entirely, we must go further than Mr. Walker, and discard the duplicate pronoun as well as the verb preceding it. A line may easily be found that would do both; for example:

> And rather muse than ask why I *request it;*

in which line the last verb may be safely adopted as a proper supplement to *entreat*, on the authority of no less a personage than Quince the carpenter, who says, "I am to *entreat you*, *request you*, and desire you,"—offering us a choice of synonymes, if not as copious as Dr. Roget * would supply, yet quite sufficient for the emergency.

From this discussion we appear to arrive at something like definite principles in reference to the subject of it.

(1) Repetition, as such, offends the taste when there seems no reason for it; and is especially to be condemned if it involves tautology, or an inappropriate and unsanctioned use of terms.

* Vide his "Thesaurus of English Words."

(2) Repetition, on the other hand, does not offend the taste, and is consequently not to be condemned, when it conduces to compactness or emphasis, or strengthens antithesis, or assists the point or turn of a sentiment, or is requisite for an intentional play upon words.

When, accordingly, any repetition in Shakespeare can be shown to fall under the first of these predicaments, the probability is that it was not the product of his pen.

If, on the other hand, a repetition can be brought under the second description, we may fairly set it down as genuine.

With regard to repetitions of a dubious character, which cannot be ranged decidedly under either class, or which admit of controversy, one safe rule may, I think, be laid down — namely, where better sense is made by the repeated word in both places than by any substitute, we shall probably be right in allowing the repetition to remain undisturbed, giving sense the victory over sound.

Before concluding the subject, I would again advert to a point of some importance in our attempts at correcting the fault under review.

Take an admitted instance of it. Everybody, we will suppose, sees the fault; no one defends the received text, which is condemned simply on account of the want of purpose and consequent bad taste in the repetition. The majority of annotators, in attempting to correct the fault, will proceed on the assumption that the supplanted phrase must bear some resemblance to the one substituted for it; but since the aimless and disagreable recurrence of words may be owing to widely varying causes, such resemblance cannot be regarded as necessary, and to seek for it indiscriminately or exclusively often misleads. So it has done, if I mistake not, in a case which I have already adduced as an undisputed example of faulty duplication. For the convenience of the reader, I will quote the lines again, which are in reply to an inquiry what it is to love: —

> "It is to be all made of fantasy,
> All made of passion, and all made of wishes;
> All adoration, duty, and *observance;*
> All humbleness, all patience and impatience;
> All purity, all trial, all *observance.*"

The critics have suggested, some *obedience*, and others *obeisance*, in place of one of the duplicate words, because these two nouns are somewhat like *observance*, in beginning, at all events, with the same syllable; not, I think, duly noticing that while neither of these corrections would furnish peculiarly appropriate sense, whichsoever of them might be selected would still keep up a disagreeable jingle, arising from the terminations of the three last lines—namely,

obedience.
impatience.
observance.

Shakespeare, we have a right to conclude, would not have given utterance to so tasteless a mixture of monotony and dissonance. The pursuit of similarity has here, in my estimation, led the critics astray.

If, leaving it out of contemplation, we assume that we have nothing to guide us in the selection either of the duplicate word to be dismissed (whether that in the third or that in the fifth line) or the word to be installed in its place, except considerations of taste, fitness, and conformity of style, we shall probably succeed better.

After making trial of several emendations that presented themselves, the following strikes me as having a slight probability in its favour :

> All adoration, duty, and observance,
> All humbleness, all patience and impatience,
> All purity, all trial, all *devotion.*

The last word accords well enough with the rest, and may easily be shown to be Shakespearian. Malcolm, in the fourth act of the tragedy of "Macbeth," enumerating the graces befitting a king, includes in the list, "mercy, lowliness, *devotion*, *patience;*" and in "Troilus and Cressida," *purity* and *devotion* are brought together in the same sentence (act iv. sc. 4).

Should we adopt the word here suggested, we by so doing should, at the same time, determine in which line to put it; for there being already a noun ending in *tion* in the first of the three lines here quoted, it would be a departure from the very principles of good taste we are insisting upon, to force upon the verse the unwelcome addition of a second noun with that ending, especially when the third line offers no such objection to receive it. *Devotion*, too, forms a better climax.

PART V.

CONCLUSION.—OBJECTIONS OBVIATED.

It is not in the nature of the case that all the attempts made in the preceding pages to restore the text of our great dramatist should prove successful, or be at once estimated at their real value, whatever that may be.

The business, however, of justly appreciating each of them has been rendered comparatively easy by my having proposed no emendation without assigning the reasons on which it is founded.

Leaving the particular alterations suggested to maintain themselves by these reasons against objections which it is impossible to foresee in their exact shape, and therefore impossible individually to obviate, I think I may venture to anticipate and try to remove a few difficulties which even the thoughtful may find in the *principles* applied to the correction of the text.

It is probable enough that an objection of a

somewhat subtile character may be raised to the very nature of the method that I have pursued in many of the most important emendations.

It may be alleged that some of the chief considerations adduced by me to prove that Shakespeare could not have written certain lines or used certain expressions as they stand in the received text, or afterwards to justify the proposed emendations of those lines, must have been unknown to the poet, and could not possibly have swayed him in the heat of composition. I have, it is true, in the prosecution of my design, frequently endeavoured to trace the natural or the habitual course and logical sequence of his ideas and expressions, with a view of proving that in a given passage his thoughts, as proceeding from a man of clear and strong head, must have unfolded themselves in a particular way, and that the passage in its received form, differing from the way indicated, could not have been written by him.

For example: in discussing the language of a line containing a question put by the physician to Macbeth, where *stuff'd* has usurped the place of *foul*, I point out not only a violation of good taste not Shakespearian, by a monotonous and disagreeable repetition, but that there is an incongruity in using the word *cleanse* in the case of anything merely *stuff'd*, which Shakespeare could not have fallen into; and that, if we look at the context, we shall find the string of questions there introduced uniformly characterised by a close correspondence between the several verbs and their objects, so that the marked deficiency of mutual adaptation between the two terms, in this one question, proves that they cannot both be genuine. From these and other facts I infer that *stuff'd* is wrong, and that *foul* is right.

Now, it may possibly be said that I am here representing the poet as expressing his thoughts with a conscious reference to principles which we have no reason to suppose he had at all in view. He probably never glanced for an instant at the circumstance that the verb *cleanse* requires a phrase expressive of pollution to follow it, or at the uncouthness of aimlessly repeating a word in the same line. But I have really made no such representation of Shakespeare's consciousness. We are all of us guided in intellectual action by principles to which we seldom make conscious reference. Our thoughts are suggested, combined, associated, and uttered, without any advertence to, nay, without any knowledge of, the principles on which these incidents depend, unless we purposely make them objects of attention. A hypothetical example will elucidate this. Our convenient friend A (by supposition) meets with a certain person in the street; that person, by having on some peculiar article of dress, brings to his mind a scene in Wales, where he first saw it worn; hence follows the recollection of the Welsh mountains; thereupon certain geological phenomena are immediately suggested; these take him to pre-historic periods—to the igneous rocks, to the earliest traces of vegetable and animal life; to the first appearance of mankind on the mutable crust of our diversified sphere; and so his ideas run on till he is landed, perhaps, in the "Vestiges of Creation," or Mr. Darwin's "Origin of Species." Through this long train of conceptions, you may trace that some were suggested by proximity, some by resemblance, some by causation; but whatever were the relations that brought them into his mind, our friend A was (a thousand to one) utterly unconscious that any such governed his thoughts, or were circumstances on which the intellectual procession depended.

So the man of genius is totally unconscious, not only, like the rest of us, of the common principles that lead on our ideal trains, but also of those subtile causes which shape, or those peculiar links which connect, his lofty or beautiful or powerful thoughts—thoughts which come and marshal themselves and depart without any law of which he is at the moment cognizant. He is unaware, for the most part, how his genius is determined to produce the clear crystal of good sense, the brilliant flashes of wit, or the richly-coloured flowers of fancy by which his writings are distinguished. But although unconscious of the principles which direct him, he obeys them, or yields to their control, or, in simpler and more accurate language, they are the *recurring ways* in which his mind spontaneously acts; and we, his readers, can often trace those connections of thought, whether common or peculiar, when they are before us in written language, of which he himself was insensible in the act of creation.

Hence, in the event of his writings being vitiated and mutilated by careless or incapable or unfaithful copyists, it is a safe and legitimate proceeding on our part to attempt, by studying the habitual connections of his ideas and the general characteristics of his genius, together with his customary phraseology, to determine whether particular sentences and expressions ascribed to him are genuine or not. But by so doing we by no means assert that he was conscious of the principles which governed the operations of his intellect. We are only dealing, as observers, with the relations we find in his uttered thoughts and with their consequences.

A man like Shakespeare, of powerful intellect and great command of language (not to complicate the subject by naming other qualities), is naturally so constituted that he cannot, so long as he is in a healthy condition of body and mind, deliberately utter anything weak, incoherent, or confused; not that he intentionally avoids weakness, incoherence, and confusion, and is conscious that he does so, but because these are not the fruits which his peculiar cast of mind yields, any more than haws are the fruit of the vine, or hips of the fig-tree.

When, therefore, you find the composition of such a man deformed by the faults just named, you may conclude with much confidence that they are patches put upon it by some external agency,—just as you would conclude if you found haws and hips on your vines and fig trees, that they had not grown there, but had been stuck on by some mischievous urchin or eccentric humorist. You would draw a very different inference from merely finding a grape discoloured, or a fig deficient in fullness and flavour.

But, passing from the question regarding consciousness, objectors may further urge that I have gone on the hypothesis of the poet's undeviating excellence and impeccability — at least in certain particulars. It may possibly be said that I have assumed him to have been always a consistent thinker and correct reasoner; to have steered clear on every occasion of absurd propositions, lame antitheses, and incongruous metaphors, and to have uniformly expressed himself in the most forcible and appropriate language : whereas he, like other writers, doubtless sometimes failed and blundered in argument, in figures, and in expression : consequently such assumptions are untenable,— and if we start from them as principles by which to judge of the received text, we shall be led into much fallacious criticism and many erroneous conclusions.

The preceding objection is not without plausibility and even weight. It may be allowed that

Shakespeare occasionally committed such errors, that such blots may be now and then found in his composition. We may be here and there crossed by the *paucis maculis quas aut incuria fudit aut humana parum cavit natura.* The admission, however, does not shake the validity of the procedure which the objection is meant to impugn. It is possible that in a thousand instances, or even in a hundred, the assumptions may fail once; and, of course, in that instance of failure I shall be attempting to correct incoherence of thought and inanity of language which really issued from his pen.

Well, what then? Where is the mischief? Let us suppose ninety-nine criticised passages (or any other proportion) out of a hundred to be restored from corruption to the state in which they originally came from his hands, and the hundredth, with all its imperfections, to be genuine, and to be erroneously improved.

What is the amount of evil? One passage is transformed from its genuine faultiness into something better, by following out the same principles which effect the restoration of ninety-nine corrupt passages to their genuine excellence. Would it be good sense to abandon the method of proceeding, and to insist on retaining the ninety and nine with all their imperfections, lest, by restoring them to their original purity, we should in a single instance substitute a greatly better reading than the author's own?

The probability is so much in favour of coming to a right result under such assumptions, that it is wise to make them, notwithstanding the slight chance of blundering into an improvement. The latter is doubtless to be deprecated, since our object ought to be the simple restoration, not the melioration, of the original text; but it is an evil, the chances of which need not disturb us if we can secure the greater good. There is, besides, another consideration of much weight. If there are incongruities and weaknesses and other faults in Shakespeare, discordant with his usual strain, and yet the genuine product of his pen, we may make ourselves almost sure that they occur in the less important parts of the dialogue. In those which are of great pith and moment, we may take it for granted that he could not fail to put forth all the powers of his mind, his clearness of discernment, his closeness of reasoning, his keen insight into the analogies of things, his vigour of conception, his richness of imagination, his almost preternatural sense of the import of words, his unparalleled command of language, and his admirable faculty of condensation; consequently, the risk of error which we incur by proceeding on the assumptions in question when we are dealing with those remarkable passages where the restoration of the genuine text is most to be desired, becomes exceedingly small.

Accordingly, I have ventured, with some confidence, to assume that in producing that masterly composition distinguished as Hamlet's soliloquy, the powers of Shakespeare's mind were fully awake, and that he could not have originated the incongruity and inconsequence of thought by which the received text in the early part of the soliloquy is deformed. I have felt similar confidence in assuming that, with an intellect at its full tension, he could not have committed those faults of incoherence of thought and awkwardness of expression which disfigure and enfeeble the taunts of Lady Macbeth when she is instigating her less resolute husband to the murder of his guest.

Widely at variance with these views is the timid reluctance of some editors and critics of Shakespeare to admit any considerable emendation, notwithstanding their acknowledgment that the text is spurious, or at least inexplicable, and although the amendment proposed is capable of enduring the most rigorous tests, as well as confessedly fits the place assigned to it. Rather than innovate, they will resort to the most strained interpretation of language, and tenaciously hold to a reading, because it has possession which could not have originated with any writer of common sense, much less with our clear and strong-minded dramatist. They fail to see how the case really stands.

Here is a book written by one of the greatest men of genius that ever lived, but handed down to us with a text so imperfect and perverted, that it contains hundreds, not to say thousands, of spurious passages. A critic takes the book in hand, and, complying with the strictest rules and conditions which can be reasonably imposed, shows irrefutably a passage to be corrupt, and proposes a way to correct it. If, unable to disprove his reasons, we refuse to adopt what is thus offered to us, we are rejecting an emendation extremely likely to be the genuine reading while it is certainly an improved one, and instead of embracing the proffered good, we are retaining a word or a sentence shown on unimpeachable grounds to be spurious. We are casting away what is proved to be very probably right, and clinging to what has no probability in its favour.

APPENDIX

APPENDIX.

ARTICLE I.

A CURSORY COMPARISON OF THE CORRUPTIONS IN SHAKESPEARE'S TEXT WHICH ARE NOTED IN THE PRECEDING COMMENTARY, WITH MODERN ERRORS OF THE PRESS.

SUCH of the readers of the foregoing treatise as have had little or nothing to do with transcribing manuscripts and printing or correcting proof-sheets, may possibly regard some of the emendations brought forward in it as extremely improbable from the magnitude of the blunders implied; in other words, from the great difference between the received text in certain passages and that which I have proposed to substitute for it. To the inexperienced in those details which are necessary before a volume in type can be placed under their eyes, it may be almost inconceivable that such great mistakes should be committed by either copyist or compositor; and if they had been committed, that they should have escaped the eyes of those coadjutors whose business it was to revise the written or printed sheets. Such readers can imagine, perhaps, that *kin* might have been inadvertently changed into *knit*, or *niece* into *near*, but are slow to apprehend the probability, or even the possibility, of *armed* being transmuted into *able*, or *fruit* into *news*.

The best way of obviating or removing an objection of this nature is to show that equally great errors are committed in the present day, when it is so much easier to avoid them.

With this view I purpose to adduce actual instances from recent works, and place them alongside some of the principal defects which I have pointed out or found already noted, and have attempted to amend, in Shakespeare. If such a parallel do not afford much novelty or instruction to the literary adept, it may amuse the uncritical reader. The comparison will be made under some disadvantages, inasmuch as it is errors of the press alone in modern books that can be cited,—that is, unintentional deviations of the printing from the manuscript, without of course the knowledge or conscious concurrence of the author; but the errors in Shakespeare to be compared with these are such as may have arisen from two sources: some of them may have originated in the printing-office, and some in the preparation of the manuscript itself.

Since there are thus two sources of corruption in the latter case, it is natural to expect the mistakes to be of a grosser or more flagrant character than the *errata* in the publications of our own time. As some set-off against this, I may here premise that a number of the modern errors of the press which I shall adduce will be taken from daily and weekly journals—publications more liable to lapses of that description than works printed and issued at leisure. Still, were we to take into view the whole of the errors in Shakespeare's plays, it might possibly appear that they were of a grosser kind than those of our modern press, newspapers included.

Whether this is really the case or not may be here, however, left undetermined, since it is not requisite for my present design to go beyond that limited number of spurious readings which I have myself made the subjects of comment, and endeavoured to correct.

All I need undertake to show is, that these are not grosser mistakes than such as are now daily committed; and that, consequently, the alterations in the text made to rectify them do not labour under any antecedent improbability on account of their magnitude.

I may, however, digress into the general remark, that the prominent difference between the errors in Shakespeare's dramatic writings and those in modern books is in their *quantity*, not in their *quality*.

If we take up a recent publication, even a newspaper, we shall probably find the mistakes of the press "few and far between:" if we take up "Macbeth," or "Hamlet," or the "Tempest," as they appear in the earliest copies, we shall perceive the defects in the text to be numerous; but if we proceed to compare the character of the two sets of errors, we shall discover the greater portion of both to be near akin. I say the greater portion, because there are in the old copies omissions and mutilations beyond remedy, which have, in the nature of the case, no counterpart in the regular tenour of modern literature. It is only between errors of a corrigible kind that any comparison can well be instituted such as I am engaged in.

The causes of this multiplicity of spurious passages in the works of our great dramatist have been already several times adverted to, and have been explained, as far as existing records supply the materials, by various commentators. From the scanty evidence accessible to us, it appears that, owing to the way in which the manuscript itself was formed previous to being placed before the compositor, many errors were occasioned by circumstances not incident to the preparation of modern works: some were committed in taking down the words from dictation or recitation; others originated in transcription; and such, when once incorporated with the text, would, in the absence or *aloofness* of the author, have little chance of being rectified at any subsequent stage. It further appears that the manuscript thus formed was often badly written, with the words much abbreviated, if not actually in shorthand; and of all the causes originating errors of the press, the illegibility of hand-writing is perhaps the most prolific and influential. When the proof-sheets are revised by the author himself, mistakes from this source can be easily rectified; but such was not the good fortune of any of the plays at present in question.

The causes which thus increased the quantity of errors in the text of Shakespeare had not, however, the same influence over their quality. The blunders and oversights committed by copyists, and compositors, and revisers, depend very much, in every age and in all countries, on the same principles,— that is to say, on the same mental defects and frailties; and hence, howsoever they are multiplied, a family resemblance is generally traceable between those that respectively deform the works of different authors, although the parties to the blunders may have been widely separated from each other in point of time and birth-place.*

* Thomas Heywood, in his "Apology for Actors," 1612 (four years before the death of Shakespeare), gives rather an amusing account of his fate amongst the printers. "The infinite faults," he says, "escaped in my book of 'Britaines Troy,' by the negligence of the printer, as the misquotations, mistaking of syllables, misplacing half-lines, coining of strange and never-heard-of words, these being without number; when I would have taken a particular account of the *errata*, the

Waiving, however, the attempt to establish or adequately illustrate the general proposition above laid down, which would require a disproportionate space here, I have in view on the present occasion, as already intimated, the less arduous task of showing that the particular errors in Shakespeare's text, which I have undertaken to deal with in the foregoing commentary, can be paralleled by errors of the press in our recent literature.

One of the most remarkable changes in the received text which I have ventured to propose, is replacing the sounding phrase *a sea of troubles*, in Hamlet's celebrated soliloquy, by the humbler expression *the seat of troubles*,—an alteration which, in its mere verbal character, is rather slight, but which seems almost violent in virtue of withdrawing the imagination from the boundless ocean and fixing it on the narrow region of the human breast.

The error, colossal as it looks, is paralleled by a mistake which occurred a few years ago in a review of one of my own works. The right reading of the passage in question was

"The *reasoner* must have been acquainted with a similar case,"

which was perverted in the review to,

"The *seamen* must have been acquainted with a similar case."

The transition from *reasoner* to *seamen* is verbally as great as from *the seat* to *a sea*.

printer answered me, he would not publish his owne dis-workmanship, but 'rather let his owne fault lye upon the necke of the author.'" If a work published under the author's eye thus contained *infinite faults*, we need not wonder that Shakespeare's works, of which a complete edition did not appear till seven years after his death, abound with the errors here described.

Almost as remarkable a change as the preceding follows in the next line of the same soliloquy: *by a poniard end them,* is put, as an amendment, in the place of *by opposing end them,* in which the disparity in meaning is not so marked, but the verbal alteration is greater. The same review, however, will furnish a tolerable match to this blunder. In citing a passage which correctly given is, "The chief cases of similarity being those of *causation,*" the review ingeniously transforms it into, "The chief cases of similarity being those of *accusation.*"

A *poniard* is not more different from *opposing* than *causation* is from *accusation;* and the difference between the two first readings becomes still less, if, as I before suggested, we take the old forms. Compare

a poynard *vice* opponing,

with

causation *vice* accusation.

I have taken occasion to adduce several singular mistakes in the tragedy of "Macbeth," all of which might be easily "followed" by "modern instances." The two I am about to cite are notable for having transformed nouns with the abstract termination *ness* in the original text (as I read it) into others with different endings and different significations, making them into concrete terms. *Blanket* is substituted for *blackness,* and *beast* for *baseness;* to which I may add an analogous instance from another play, where *beauty* has replaced *blackness.* The two first may be met by a single example which I took down from a newspaper in the current year, presenting us with *gentlemen* instead of *gentleness*; and the last is matched in point of grossness by a misprint in another journal of *guardians* for *gentleman.*

In the same tragedy the perversion of *evade it* into *inhabit* is fully equalled by a corruption which crept into one of my own volumes, and was not detected either by the reviser at the printing office, or by the author who carefully went through the proofs; — an oversight the more extraordinary, as the substituted word (like *inhabit* above quoted) completely ruined the sense; *monstrous* was put in the place of *monotonous.*

When proposing to make the change (in Lady Macbeth's strong expostulation with her husband) of *love* into *liver,* I could not help anticipating that many wise heads would be shaken at so bold a proposal and so derogatory a descent from the tender passion. Lately taking up Emerson's "Conduct of Life," I came to the following passage on a somewhat different subject, where the verbal transmutation is not less, and where the chasm between the meanings of the right and the wrong reading is, to say the least, equally wide:

> "Not Antoninus, but a poor washerwoman, said, 'The more trouble the more *lion*; that's my principle.'" *

Linen transformed into *lion,* is certainly as extraordinary a metamorphosis as *liver* into *love,* whether we regard it as typographical or substantial.

Another error in this great tragedy is so singular, that it is difficult to find any analogous blunder in recent publications, although there is no lack of equal ones. *Time and the hour,* by a very natural lapse, has been substituted for *Time's sandy hour,* — a corruption, however, not surpassing one I met with lately in a newspaper, which, having occasion to mention the eminent political economist Thomas *Tooke,* called him Mr. *Toolie.*

* London Edition, 1860, p. 224.

The next example I have to cite brings before us a name which all Englishmen, and especially all soldiers (if the sentiment can admit of degrees) delight to honour. Miss Florence Nightingale, in a letter not long ago addressed to the chairman (I think) of some meeting of volunteer rifle-men, liberally offered to present to the corps a *pair of colours.* The report of this offer in the newspaper wherein I first saw it, converted the intended gift into a *fair of colours,* which future commentators, proceeding on the principle that no change should be made in the text when any possible meaning can be extorted from it, will doubtless explain, as designed by that distinguished lady, to signify a fancy fair and its lucrative proceeds; such fairs (they will add) having been often held in those days (sometimes under the denomination of bazaars) for benevolent or public-spirited purposes.

This is not a bad, although an easily detected, instance of those simple substitutions of single letters which make such disproportionate havoc with an author's meaning; and as it concerns what are eminently destined to be the playthings of the wind, it will help to keep in countenance my proposed transformation in "Julius Cæsar" of the *lane* into the *vane* of children.

A single line in the tragedy of "Coriolanus" is restored to its genuine reading (as I think it) by two alterations; one is a substitution of *trump* for *tomb,* the other of *child's* for *chair*; neither of which constitutes a greater difference than I observed a short time ago in a country journal, where *administrative purposes* had been supplanted by *administrative paupers.* And if it be objected by any reader that two errors ought in this case to appear in the same sentence, otherwise there can be no complete parallel, I can meet the objection by citing the following passage from another journal: " The *fleet* of the British government is at this moment *winning* its way across the waters of the Atlantic," where *fleet* is printed instead of *fiat*, and *winning* instead of *winging*.

I have been somewhat at a loss to match the perversion of the *quintessence of white* into a princess — *the princess of pure white*, as the received text gives it. On looking over some notes, however, which I had made on errors of the press, I found a case in point, so far at least as dealing with a high potentate can render it so. A journal in the present year (1861) unsexes Louis Napoleon's Consort, and styles her *the Emperor Eugenie*. The reader will notice perhaps a small difference, which is however of no account in the comparison,— namely, that the first error makes a princess, the second unmakes one.

The last name reminds me that I have yet to find a counterpart to the blunder which has so injuriously (*spretæ injuria formæ*) discarded the attitude of the Queen of Beauty, transmuting *the shrinking Venus* of the genuine text into *the shrine of Venus*, which may mean anything.* Abundance of equal transformations offer themselves, but not one of them constitutes a notable parallel. In sub-

* A literary humorist might insist, for example, on its referring to the *scrinium unguentarium* of Venus, of which Rich gives a representation from a painting found at Pompeii. See the article Scrinium, in his excellent "Illustrated Companion to the Latin Dictionary and Greek Lexicon,"—a work which it would have cheered Locke's heart to see, so well does it correspond with what he recommends in his "Essay on Human Understanding," and enforces in a section, from which I can afford space for only a brief extract: "Toga, tunica, pallium, are words easily translated by gown, coat, and cloak; but we have thereby no more true ideas of the fashion of those habits amongst the Romans than we have of the faces of the tailors who made them. Such things as these, which the eye distinguishes by their shapes, would be best let into the mind by draughts made of them." Book III. Chap. xi. § 25.

stance, if not in form, the following error of the press may serve the turn:—It is mentioned in the "Life of Edward Forbes" as having occurred in a paper of his printed in the "Edinburgh Philosophical Journal," and as having been purely the consequence of his illegible hand-writing. The correct manuscript reading was "Natural History *unlike her sister sciences;*" which was printed in the journal "Natural History *under its sub-sciences.*"

Like this gross corruption, the two last mis-readings pointed out in Shakespeare were owing, I have little doubt, to the illegible condition of the manuscript.

In the reprint of Gosson's "Schoole of Abuse" a curious error occurs: "He that goes to sea must smel of the ship, and that which sayles into *poets* wil savour of pitch:" in which, I presume, *poets* was intended for *ports**; and as only a single letter is in question, the instance may serve to corroborate the *prop* which in "Cymbeline," by an equally slight change, I have ventured to substitute for the *crop.*

Shakespeare's works do not exhibit many mistakes in compound words, or I have overlooked them; for, in the course of the preceding commentary, I have corrected only two: I have restored *winter-fend,* which had been perverted into *winter-ground,* and *counterwait,* which had been perverted into *countermand.*

My memoranda of modern errors of the press afford me only a single analogous one: "*heir-apparent* was lately transmuted by a respectable journal into *heir-apparel;* which I conceive leaves neither of the preceding blunders in Shakespeare's text "unfellowed."

The fault or corruption which I have separately con-

* The reprint quoted from is by the Shakespearian Society, p. 14, but whether the blunder is owing to the old or the modern typographer I am not able to say.

sidered under the title of verbal repetition, I do not find at all common in modern publications. My notes indeed contain only two instances of it. Its rarity compared with its former frequency is owing, I conceive, partly to the stricter supervision which the proof-sheets have now to undergo, and partly to the other circumstances, before detailed, affecting generally the quantity of errors in Shakespeare's text. In one of the instances I have just referred to, the word *author* is printed twice — once instead of *advocate;* in the other, there is fact + fact instead of fact + part.

To those authors who are in the habit of making extracts, or of copying their own compositions for the press, this species of blunder must, I conceive, be familiar, —at least if their experience tallies with my own. As a case in point I may mention that, while preparing the present treatise, I inadvertently fell one evening into a palpable error of this description; and although I reperused at the time what I had written, I did not detect the oversight till next morning, when the intellectual film (*i. e.* pre-occupation of mind) which seems occasionally to dim the discernment as to certain objects, and not to others, had been dissipated. It was in transcribing a passage from "Cymbeline," in which the following lines occur, that I made the false step: —

"I have heard of riding wagers,
Where horses have been nimbler than the *sands*
That run i' the *clocks* by half." Act iii. sc. 2.

Instead of writing *clocks* in the third of these lines, I repeated *sands* from the second line — an incident worth mentioning only as an illustration of a real and frequent source of literary mistakes.*

* In the quotation from "Cymbeline" I have adopted the emendation of the Perkins folio, viz. "that run i' the clocks *by half*,"

The proneness to this sort of iteration is rather curiously exhibited in a slight error of the press which I accidentally remarked in Bowdler's "Family Shakespeare;" and the same error may be cited as showing another thing worthy of notice, that the repetition is sometimes made (paradoxical as the statement may be) *before* the original word repeated, as in the line which has already been the subject of comment—

"To seek thy *help* by beneficial *help*,"

where it is the first *help* that has been thrust into the line by the second.

So in the passage I have referred to as misprinted in Bowdler—

"*Yoo* shall have me assisting you in all,
But will you *woo* this wild cat?"
Taming of the Shrew, Act i. sc. 2.

---

instead of the received reading, "that run i' the clocks' behalf," notwithstanding the contemptuous denunciation of it by Mr. Singer, who too often discredits criticism by bitterness of spirit and intemperance of language, which are never the aids, although frequently the substitutes, of fact and argument.

The sound of both expressions in pronunciation being very commonly the same, the question as to the genuine reading is to be decided by propriety and usage alone. To call an hour-glass *a clock* has nothing forced about it, especially in a writer who tells us "larks are ploughmen's clocks;" and to say that the sands in it are not so nimble as horses *by half*, or to keep strictly to the text, that horses are nimbler *by half* than the sands in the glass, is only to employ a form of speech exceedingly prevalent amongst the people. "Better by half," "quicker by half," "prettier by half," are common phrases. An article in a Magazine (dated Dec. 1861), which I have just taken up, uses the expression, "too fast by half."

On the other hand, to speak of the sands of an hour-glass running *in behalf of* the clock, is, to say the least, strained; and the difficulty of telling exactly what it means, if we may judge from Mr. Singer's attempt, is not small. He explains the sense to be that the sands run *in lieu of*, or *on the part of*, the clock; expressions which are so far from being always equivalent, that they are in this case diverse in signification.

Where it is evident that *woo* by a back stroke has transformed the first *you* into an orthographical likeness of itself, passing over the two other *you's* without touching them; as the lightning sometimes wreaks its fire on one privileged mortal (according to the poet*) and takes no heed of his neighbours.

Occasionally very curious blunders arise from a misarrangement of the type. I do not recollect noticing any such in Shakespeare; there are none at least in the passages I have dealt with; but it may be worth while adducing one or two instances in modern printing, were it only to show the possibility of committing gross oversights, even with our improved methods of supervision, and thence to infer a similar liability with inferior appliances two or three hundred years ago.

In a newspaper last July, I remarked a most extraordinary passage, viz. "*an inch oateact*," of which at the first glance I could make nothing at all. It looked most like *an inch oatcake*, but as that article of human sustenance is not usually measured with a foot-rule and had no connexion with the context, I looked again, and after a little perplexity saw that the dislocation of the type had revolutionised the meaning. When the letters were properly marshalled, the right reading proclaimed itself to be *an inchoate act*, and thus escaped from the dominion of mensuration and the category of eatables.

The celebrated "Essays and Reviews," amidst the heavy blows aimed at it, will not be damaged by my noticing a misarrangement of this kind in the seventh edition of the work †, where the letter *s* (whatever the authors may

* "Or favour'd man by touch ethereal slain."—Thomson.

† Page 400.

have done) has certainly wandered out of bounds in *reason*, that word being printed *reaons*.

Sometimes there is a clandestine exchange of letters between an upper and a lower line, which is perplexing enough till you detect the illicit barter. Knight's Pocket Shakespeare (1851) presents us with as simple an instance of this as can well be found:

> "I dreading that her purpose
> Was of more danger, did compound for her
> *T* certain stuff, which, being ta'en, would cease
> *A*he present power of life."
>
> *Cymbeline*, act v. sc. 5.

The initial letters of the two last lines have so obviously changed places, that I scarcely need point it out. The marvel is how an error so gross could escape correction.

The occurrence of such extraordinary errors as the preceding may in some measure facilitate to incredulous readers the reception of my theory as to the origin of that strange blunder with the word comma, which disfigures a passage in "Hamlet" and which I have attributed to the incorporation of a marginal direction into the text. I must candidly own however that my very desultory search has not met with any similar fusion in modern literature: but if oversights are made in the present day, such as those last described, there cannot be much difficulty in supposing the one in question to have been committed nearly three centuries ago, especially since the collateral circumstances so well combine to account for it, and the proposed emendation so completely fills and fits the vacancy created by turning out the intruding words.

Besides, although I have no corresponding blunder to adduce in the literature of our own times, the classical and biblical scholar knows that amidst abundance of errors of all sorts, it has happened sufficiently often to show such blending not to be particularly difficult — that the text of ancient manuscripts has absorbed into itself the marginal glosses of critics and commentators with much more serious effect on the meaning than is exhibited in the case before us.

ARTICLE II.

NOTE A, SUPPLEMENTARY TO PAGE 116.

WHEN I was proposing an emendation in the 1st act of "Cymbeline" and the 7th sc., it was an oversight on my part not to advert to another error, a few lines farther on, where the speaker is affecting to be perplexed how to account for the alleged faithlessness of Posthumus to his wife and his defection to an ordinary trull. He goes on to say,

> "It cannot be i' the eye; for apes and monkeys,
> 'Twixt two such shes, would chatter this way, and
> Contemn with mows the other: Nor i' the judgment;
> For idiots, in this case of favour, would
> Be wisely definite: Nor i' the appetite;
> Sluttery to such neat excellence oppos'd,
> Should make desire * *vomit* emptiness,
> Not so allured to feed."

The commentators, with the exception of Tyrwhitt, strangely enough, receive the eccentric phrase *vomit emptiness* without demur, and earnestly set themselves to explain it as they best can. Notwithstanding all their efforts, they do not succeed in proving that it has any appropriate significance here.

Malone, indeed, has shown that it describes sufficiently well an incident of sea-sickness, to which I need not more

* It may be well to mention, that *desire* is to be pronounced here as a trisyllable, as if written (as it frequently was), *de-si-er*.

particularly allude; but admitting *that,* we want to know the propriety of its appearance in the passage before us.

Let us examine the exposition of it furnished by one of the principal critics.

"Iachimo," says Dr. Johnson, "in this counterfeited rapture, has shown how the *eyes* and the *judgment* would determine in favour of Imogen, comparing her with the present mistress of Posthumus, and proceeds to say that appetite too would give the same suffrage. *Desire,* says he, when it approached *sluttery,* and considered it in comparison with *such neat excellence,* would not only be *not so allured to feed,* but, seized with a fit of loathing, *would vomit emptiness,* would feel the convulsions of disgust, though being unfed, it had no object."

Now, allowing this interpretation to be correct, its own incoherence betrays that the passage is spurious. The able critic quite overlooks the requirements of the personification. A *man* may first long for a thing and then loathe it, but to describe *desire* itself as loathing is to make it "deny its nature;" commit contradictory acts; "empty itself of its identity and become the opposite of what it is."

The other terms used by the poet in speaking of *desire* are correct enough: he represents it as susceptible of being allured and capable of feeding; in which there is nothing self-contradictory, and we have on that account as well as on general grounds a right to suppose that the incoherent description of a passion, the very essence of which is to *long,* as in a fit of repugnance and retching, cannot be his.

All that is needed to extricate Shakespeare and his readers out of this embarrassment, appears to me to be an exceedingly slight verbal alteration. The poet, as I read him, intended to say that sluttery should make Desire prefer going without a repast to feeding on such diet as that described. This meaning would be effectively brought out by the substitution of a single word sufficiently resembling the spurious one. We have only to read,

> Sluttery to such neat excellence oppos'd,
> Should make desire *covet* emptiness,
> Not so allured to feed.

The reader will discover for himself without my assistance how readily *covet* might be perverted into the received reading. The error might have originated in the similarity of the two sounds, or it might have arisen from an accidental transposition of the first and third letters in setting up the type, turning *covet* into *vocet.* This done, the blunder as it now stands would be virtually achieved, for any reviser coming upon such a word would inevitably convert it into *vomit.*

ARTICLE III.

NOTE B, SUPPLEMENTARY TO PAGE 118.

I HAVE intimated in a note at the foot of p. 118 that there are reasons for altering the word *feature*, in the passage quoted in that page, to *figure*. I will here add that there are also grounds for substituting in a subsequent line another epithet in the place of *brief*.

That the questions may be brought fully before the reader, I will again quote the passage as I have corrected it in the page referred to.

Iachimo says that Posthumus was

"sitting sadly
He ring us praise our loves of Italy,
For BEAUTY that made barren the swell'd boast
Of him that best could speak; for FEATURE laming
The shrinking Venus, or straight-pight Minerva,
Postures beyond brief nature: for CONDITION
A shop of all the qualities that man
Loves woman for: besides that hook of wiving
FAIRNESS which strikes the eye."

Here — set forth with almost the formality of a puritan's sermon — there are four distinct topics of eulogy, or topics which ought to be and were doubtless intended to be distinct; beauty, feature, condition, and complexion: but since female beauty, as ordinarily regarded, lies in the countenance, it seems an unskilful repetition to introduce *feature* afterwards as a separate topic: it is a sort of cross classification. What however is a greater fault is that the speaker proceeds to append to the latter term circumstances not at all congruous with its import. He says in fact that the Italian boasters on this occasion praised their mistresses for *features* which made even the Venus and the Minerva, in their respective attitudes, appear lame. Surely while the beautiful features of one woman may so surpass those of another as to reduce the latter to plainness in the comparison, they cannot cause the inferior fair one to wear the appearance of lameness in any attitude she may assume. The two things have no connexion. Feature consequently is not here the right phrase. The whole train of thought requires the mention of an attribute distinct from beauty of countenance and harmonising with what follows. Such a one we have in *figure.* I propose to read

for *figure* laming
The shrinking Venus or straight-pight Minerva,

making even these much admired forms look lame in the comparison. The change implied by this correction of the received text, of *figure* into the corrupt reading *feature*, can furnish no reasonable ground for demur, since greater blunders are every day committed.

Let us now turn to the word *brief,* the objection to which as an epithet applied to *nature* is that it is difficult to attach a precise signification to it. We can understand what the poet intends when he tells us that the exquisite postures of the two statues are beyond nature, but when he speaks of *brief* nature, the meaning is no longer clear; the objects before our intellectual vision seem to vacillate; and when we call to mind that Shakespeare is not in the habit of using epithets or designations without a precise and special significance, we may feel tolerably sure that *brief*, which cannot be wrested by the greatest ingenuity into a satisfactory acceptation, did not come from him.

It is not easy to find an adjective that will suit the place. The poet evidently meant to say that the attitudes of the Venus and the Minerva excel in gracefulness the postures of untutored nature. They are such as spring from cultivation and refinement. To express this meaning with due observance of the rhythm, we have only monosyllables to turn to, so that our choice of epithets is exceedingly narrow. Since a limiting rather than a characterising term is required, *mere* prefixed to *nature* might do, were it not so totally unlike *brief* both in sound and form. I would therefore suggest another adjunct similar in meaning to *mere*, but more resembling the spurious word in its component letters. *Bare* nature would, it appears to me, express all that the occasion requires or the poet intended; and it agrees in its predominant initial sounds with the word it would displace.

If this be adopted along with the other corrections which I have suggested and explained, the passage will run thus:

for *figure* laming,
The *shrinking* Venus and straight-pight Minerva,
Postures beyond *bare* nature.

Compare this with the received text:

"for *feature* laming,
The *shrine of* Venus and straight-pight Minerva,
Postures beyond *brief* nature."

It is needless, I conceive, to do more than mention that Theobald proposed *stature* instead of *feature;* and that Warburton, dissenting from this, defended the received reading, by the assertion that it meant *proportion of parts,* which Theobald, he added, did not understand.* Since

* Boswell's Malone, vol. xiii. p. 213.

this assertion is not accompanied by any proof, it is sufficient to say that I never met with the term so used in Shakespeare or anywhere else, and doubt much whether any writer was ever guilty of such a misapplication of language. *Stature* as suggested by Theobald is quite out of place, that term being limited to height.

LONDON
PRINTED BY SPOTTISWOODE AND CO.
NEW-STREET SQUARE

www.ingramcontent.com/pod-product-compliance
Lightning Source LLC
Chambersburg PA
CBHW020343030726
47496CB00007B/1980

* 9 7 8 3 3 3 7 0 5 5 9 9 8 *